The Kabbalistic Mirror of Genesis

"An amazing book—boy does it have chutzpah!"

"A gifted artist who has a deep contemporary understanding of Jewish mystical wisdom, David Chaim Smith takes us into the domain where zero is one, where the all is nothing, and where the creative moment is constantly renewing itself. *The Kabbalistic Mirror of Genesis* is not a book simply to read but to contemplate and live with."

"A unique mystical voice out of a Blakean tradition, *The Kabbalistic Mirror of Genesis* is a mind-expanding spiritual text that will both clarify and transform you. Smith has rethought biblical basics from the ground up ('with-beginningness') providing insights into the profound depths of mind, perception, reality, life, creativity, luminosity, and transcendence. . . . This is kabbalistic commentary from a living practitioner that will help us immeasurably to help heal the world."

The Kabbalistic Mirror of Genesis

COMMENTARY ON THE FIRST THREE CHAPTERS

DAVID CHAIM SMITH

Inner Traditions
Rochester, Vermont • Toronto, Canada

Inner Traditions
One Park Street
Rochester, Vermont 05767
www.InnerTraditions.com

Originally published in the United Kingdom in 2010 by Daat Press under the title
The Kabbalistic Mirror of Genesis: Commentary on Genesis 1–3

Library of Congress Cataloging-in-Publication Data

Smith, David Chaim, author.
   The kabbalistic mirror of Genesis : commentary on the first three chapters /
David Chaim Smith.
      pages cm
   Includes bibliographical references and index.
   ISBN 978-1-62055-463-0 (paperback) — ISBN 978-1-62055-464-7 (ebook)
1. Bible. Genesis I-III—Commentaries. 2. Cabala. I. Title.
BS1235.53.S65 2015
222'.1106—dc23

                                                                    2015003873

Printed and bound in the United States.

10   9   8   7   6   5   4   3   2

Text design by Priscilla H. Baker and layout by Virginia Scott Bowman
This book was typeset in Garamond Premier Pro and Gill Sans with Goudy
Oldstyle, Albertus, and Poetica used as display typefaces

CONTENTS

I could be bounded in a nutshell, and count myself a king of infinite space—were it not that I have bad dreams.

WILLIAM SHAKESPEARE, *HAMLET*

Introduction

Hidden within the first three chapters of Genesis rests one of the greatest jewels of Western mystical literature. Proper appreciation of this is rare. For millennia religious literalism has dominated the role of the Bible, imprisoning its subtle inner wisdom within the most coarse and superficial aspects of the narrative. Generations have been led to believe that Genesis 1–3 is only a primitive proto-cosmic history and mythological explanation of the human moral disposition. Multitudes of sincere would-be spiritual aspirants have been sidetracked and frustrated by what seems to be a religious fairy tale. One way that this tendency might be explained is that it is like a child's version of a mature statement. Drawing the mature implications of this material out into the light is this book's objective.

There will always be a minority who wish to advance the text beyond the vestiges of religious mythology. This requires a willingness to accept that its ultimate meaning cannot be contained by words, and can only be hinted at through esoteric analysis. This begins as the text is accepted as pure metaphor, an obscure "twilight language," which obliquely hints at its definitive content. This can point us in the direction of the incomprehensible mystery that transcends the conventional limitations of time and space. The esoteric tradition requires this intention, so the mind can be directed toward a new way of being that radically transforms the meaning of what it is to be human.

The best way for a largely secular audience to approach the kabbalistic wisdom of Genesis is to set aside all notions about what kabbalah is and start afresh by examining it with a new sensibility. This requires that basic foundation principles be revisited and new questions asked. This book asserts an uncommon view that will challenge exoteric as well as esoteric assumptions about the creative process and perception. Without provocation of this type, the mystical content of Genesis will remain buried under a mountain of mythological and religious detritus, which is absolutely superfluous to the core message of the text.

The mystical content of the first three chapters of Genesis is unlocked with a key that all kabbalists know well. It is an esoteric code of ten interactive attributes called the ten sefirot, collectively known as the Tree of Life, which articulate the manifestation of the creative process. The sefirot guide inquiry into the Divine nature and science of creativity. The vision glimpsed through the window of the sefirot reveals what creativity is, not just what it does, which is a radical departure from the exoteric religious agenda.

The mainstream view of the sefirot is that they are mediating agents between Divine essence and the differentiated functions of creation. This implies a subtle degree of separation between creator and creation. An alternative to this schism is based on radical unity that manifests as a paradox.

The sefirot certainly are the template through which creative diversity manifests; however, to understand this, it must be clear that Divinity is absolutely pervasive and negates the separate existence of any apparent limitation or boundary. The sefirot manifest infinite variation without ever diminishing the sublime nature of their unity. The wisdom of the sefirot is that wholeness is never deflected by the appearance of its apparent diversity; on the contrary, it is glorified by it.

The sefirot are ten for very important reasons. The numerical cycle 1–10 is the basis of all numerical relationships. It begins with 1, which is wholeness itself. The esoteric wisdom behind 1 is that it is equal with zero. Wholeness arises without ever departing from the expanse of potentiality which zero alludes to. This is what kabbalists refer to as "simple" Divine unity. It holds no distinction between everything and nothingness. Divine unity is all-inclusive and yet totally continuous with open possibility. This is symbolized as the numerical sequence culminates in the number 10, as the 1 returns to the primal zero that no number ever leaves. The 10 reveals that the silent womb of zero rests as the heart of all numbers, nourishing all their activities. It is the absolute perfection of wholeness beyond beginning and end, which is the lifeblood of the sefirot. The *Tikkuney Zohar* states:

> One, but not in counting. Highest of the High, secret of secrets, altogether beyond the reach of thought. (*Tikkuney Zohar*)

There is a difference between the numerical understanding of 1, which is a concept relative to calculation and measurement, and radical unity that transcends relativity. The *Sefer Yetzirah* asks:

> Before One what can be counted? (*Sefer Yetzirah*)

This quotation leaves the mind suspended in an open question that is pregnant with unfettered possibility. Unity is literally inconceivable. It is beyond any conception the mind can fabricate about it. If unity becomes concretized into the concept of a Divine "One," then a problem emerges: the mind will seek to reify and fabricate a concept about the Divine in order to try to grasp it. The One will then be fixated upon as a solid coherent idea, and it can no longer assert its open mystery. This would be no different from what is done with any ordinary mental object. If Divine unity is approached as an ordinary object, the opportunity to surrender to profound wisdom becomes completely lost.

The mystical understanding of unity goes beyond contrasting notions of being and nonbeing. The basis of normative exoteric theology is that god* (the One) is a "real" Supreme Being that exists. Belief in what is real automatically excludes what is unreal. This allows both being and nonbeing to become reified as solid concepts. The only way to transcend this is to cultivate faith in the fathomless depth of Divinity that passes beyond these habits of conventional perception. This is evident in the following quote from the thirteenth-century kabbalist Azriel of Gerona:

> You may ask: How did being arise from nothingness? Is there not an immense difference between being and nothingness? The answer is as follows: Being is in nothingness in the mode of nothingness, and nothingness is in being in the mode of being. Nothingness is being, and being is nothingness. The mode of being as it arises from nothingness is called faith. Faith applies neither to visible comprehensible being nor to invisible incomprehensible nothingness. It applies to the nexus of being and nothingness. Being does not stem from nothingness alone but rather from being and nothingness together. They are One in the simplicity of absolute undifferentiation. Our limited minds cannot grasp this, for it joins infinity. (*Derekh Ha Emunah ve Derekh ha Kefirah*)

Conventional perception is based on the division between a perceiving subject and its perceived objects. Objects of perception arise internally through emotions and thoughts, and externally through the physical senses. Regardless of whether this process arises internally or externally, conventional perception always fabricates solid conceptions

---

*There are 3 possible spellings for the word *god*. The most deferential is the Orthodox Jewish spelling, which is G-d. This treatment avoids using the word in full because the divine name must not be pronounced, even internally. The standard secular spelling is *God*. This treatment capitalizes the word assuming that *God* is an entity (either actual or mythological) and is treated like a proper categorical name. The spelling in *The Kabbalistic Mirror of Genesis* is intentionally spelled in lowercase to indicate that *god* is a mere conceptual designation and mental construct fabricated by the mind. This becomes a nontheistic gesture that cuts through the other assumptions and all their implications.

that create separations. The divisions between the subject and its objects are endless. Each moment of conception is an ocean of fragmentation that forces the mind to relate to phenomena in terms of differences. When the universe is only made up of differences, then unity becomes obscured and obstructed, and consciousness becomes lost among a confusing morass of separate pieces that seem to have nothing to do with one another. Ironically, this even happens while conceptualizing about the very unity that includes the conceptualizing mind within it.

The division between the self that knows and the object that is known is the basis of all conflict. Their confrontation produces a war that is fought to assert the vain myth of independent existence. Whatever the self takes as real is accepted and whatever falls outside of its grasp is rejected. The mind even fixates and reifies itself as an object ("I" can think about "me"). Thus we even enter into war with the idea of ourselves. This is what the mind does, which prevents any recognition of what the mind is. Because subject and object validate each other, "I think, therefore I am" will immediately be followed by "what I experience is real because I have experienced it." Here an important question can be asked: Is freedom from division possible?

The use of the term "Divine" in this commentary does not imply belief in a creator god. Belief in a god reifies the biggest and most comprehensive mental object that can be grasped. It assumes such a vast scope that the individual mind can become lost within it. Such immersion has a mystical dimension, but it is not the same as freedom. The god concept always remains a concept. This concretization of unity is the basis of theism. Theism is highly problematic for many mystics, in that all theistic systems reify some conception about the Divine. Western theological systems are monotheistic, which hold the idea that god is a complete unity.

Unity is more than a mere gathering of parts. It is wholeness itself, in which all aspects express a common essential nature. In this sense there are really no such things as "parts," nor is there even such a thing as a "whole." This is made explicit by the Baal Shem Tov, founder of the Chassidic tradition:

> If a person grasps a "part" of unity he grasps the whole, and the opposite is also true. (*Keter Shem Tov*)

In the view of the most radical mysticism, neither the whole nor any part can be said to have independent existence. To say that something exists independently presumes autonomy, and thus tangible reality. The mechanism behind this assertion pervades the conception of both the "positive" state of being as well as the "negative" state of nothingness. Mysticism provides a way out of this dilemma by suggesting ways of knowing that are not dependent upon discursive conceptuality at all. Instead, a resonance is cultivated from the deep contemplation of esoteric symbols. This "mental aroma" is the basis of gnostic inquiry, and this book asserts that the true role of the first three chapters of Genesis is to provide requisite symbology for this opportunity.

Contrasts differentiate the apparitional field, but from the view of radical unity this is not a problem. Only mental attachments that reify phenomena are a problem. Mental fixations can never "ruin" unity; they merely conceal it. The essential nature of unity cannot ever be diminished; at worst it can only be obscured. Human beings can counteract this tendency through the aspiration to spirituality. The desire for freedom is strengthened every time the longing for what is whole is recalled. Holding unity as the highest is the subject of the Jewish prayer called the *Shema*. It is a declaration of what is actually worth having faith in:

> Hear O Israel, YHVH, our God, YHVH is Unity.

It is obvious that the biblical text utilizes theistic language. However, this is not a problem for mystics if the challenge inherent in all mental activity is faced directly. All phenomena rest equally in the vast expanse of wholeness. Contemplation of this can be directly applied to the seemingly impenetrable theism of biblical language. If all phenomena are held as equally sublime, then all fragmentary views are irrelevant. To seek the heart of the Divine is to pass beyond belief in categorization. No words or ideas can block inquiry if the view beyond divisions is authentically sought and cultivated.

Essentialist monism (the esoteric extension of theism) holds the Divine to be an omnipresent undifferentiated expanse that nullifies all separateness, but it is still reified as a "Oneness." This view denies that any of the realms of creation have a true existence at all apart from their inclusion within the Divine godhead. It holds that phenomena are illusory, yet the Divine basis of that illusion is ultimately real. The eternal reality inhabits the temporary illusion as a universal "soul," which is believed to be ultimately enduring. In this view it is believed that if we immerse ourselves in this essential soul we will be unified with eternal life.

The Divine godhead is held by monists to be the equalizing basis of all energy, matter, and consciousness. The monistic conception of the Divine is undifferentiated, but always emphasizes either an ultimate state of being or nonbeing. When a system becomes locked within these extremes it can no longer be free and open. This mistake is made by kabbalists who hold the essence of Divinity to be a "negative potentiality" or "negative limitless light." This is the view of many of the schools of Hermetic Qabbalah, which often hold views based on negative essentialism.

Being and nonbeing are the extreme poles of ontological categorization. They are conceptual categories that give the intellect the illusion that it can understand what is going on. They seek to mark phenomena (or the lack of them) with a seal of finality based on definition. Being and nonbeing are like prisons, which represent the frontiers of rational human thought. Can there be anything more indicative of the limitations of human conceptual assumptions than the categories that mark whether something "is" or "is not"?

Each extreme stance can only be defined in contrast to the other. A state of being is only real because it is believed that it can be proven not to be unreal. Neither category can be proven by itself; its contrasting opposite is automatically implicit. Ironically, esoteric monism and exoteric dualism both share a reliance on reification. Both depend upon concrete conceptions of the absolute at the expense of a free wisdom beyond contrivances. The freedom at stake is the most basic nobility of the mind that all human beings can have access to. Most people intuit this freedom, and this book demonstrates that Genesis 1–3 is an instruction on how to appreciate this.

The view offered here may seem like a type of monism at first, but it is radically different. The key is understanding how the mind's nature can be an invitation into the freedom of open Divinity. Any examination of the Divine is actually an examination of the mind. What the mind does is always limited, but what it is is beyond any extreme or definition.

Genesis 1–3 is a complete model of the predicament of the mind. It begins with an examination of the common denominator of the essence and function of all phenomena contained in the Bible's first word: the Divine purity called Ain Sof (the infinite). This sublime potentiality is the lifeblood of all creative expression. Approaching the mystery of Ain Sof is the sole quest of this commentary. Its investigation poses the greatest challenge the mind can meet, which is recognition of its own Divine nature.

Part One of this book will articulate the vision of the sefirot in detail. With the limitless dynamism of B'reshit as its basis, the pattern of the sefirot will emerge through a detailed kabbalistic analysis of each aspect of the creation narrative. This will involve deconstructing each line with esoteric methods derived from the oral teachings of kabbalah.

Part Two of the book will examine the Edenic allegory, whose symbolism probes the question of how the mind either reveals or conceals its Divine nature. It poses questions that the spiritual search for meaning must end up asking: What is the basic nobility and value of our nature? What are the obstacles that prevent its recognition? What are the consequences of remaining in ignorance? Chapters 2 and 3 of Genesis articulate the disparity between the Divine nature of consciousness and the obscuring tendencies of its habits. With this in mind, a radical in-depth reassessment of its content can begin from the Bible's first word.

Appendix 1 offers a complete kabbalistic synopsis of the three chapters and their symbolism. It provides an invaluable overview and should be referred to as the complexities of the work become apparent. Employing graphic representation, appendix 2 looks at five basic contexts of the creative impulse using the Divine Names in Genesis and their derivatives.

PART I

WINDOW OF
MANIFESTATION

1

THE ESSENTIAL NATURE

OF CREATIVITY

The First Word of Genesis

With-beginningness Elohim created the heavens and the earth.
(Gen. 1:1)

The first word of the Bible in Hebrew is *B'reshit*. This word is usually translated with the phrase "In the beginning," but the interpretative translation "with-beginningness" is preferred here. In Hebrew the letter *bet* (B') is a prefix, which signifies "in" or "with." The word *Reshit* refers to a continual state of becoming. This is the condition that all things are "in." B'reshit is the dynamic nature of creativity that presents total possibility. It is always unfolding fresh, new, and unique. The continual beginning is the volatile and playful disposition that can do or be anything, which displays itself as everything.

When properly understood, B'reshit constitutes a direct assault on all conventional assumptions about the solidity of substance, the linear cohesiveness of time, and the integrity of thought. Conventional perception assumes that moments in time, appearances in space, and individual thoughts are separate, unrelated, random occurrences. The

13

wisdom of B'reshit attacks this by asserting the changeless basis of continual change.

The primordial dynamism of B'reshit is evident in the relentlessness of perception. Considering the "texture" of cognition is helpful in appreciating this. Ordinary perception is an ever-changing ocean of transformation. Waves of thought arise and fall back onto themselves, following an unquestioned and unexamined continuum. When an attempt is made to grasp a thought or feeling, the perceived moment and its contents immediately slip away into the next moment. The next moment always presents itself in a subtly different manner than the last. As this occurs, the moment that was originally sought has vanished before it could even be glimpsed. Neither the content nor context of any moment of perception is the fortress of security that it is assumed to be. The artifice of perception erodes on contact with any attempt to investigate it. The only conclusion that can be made is that the unfolding of perceptual events is not a static parade of frozen moments to be grasped at one by one; it is a constant, uncatchable, and elusive barrage.

Exoteric religion interprets the Bible's first word as an indication of creation "ex nihilo." In the proto-historical mythology a distinction is made between "before" and "after" creation. In the mystical sense, this separation is nullified by the equalizing nature of Divinity, which goes beyond all distinctions. It is asserted by the essential nature of B'reshit, which equalizes all divisions with the wisdom of pure creativity. The wisdom of B'reshit is a "Beginningness" that cannot be experienced or known in any conventional sense. Ordinary perception cannot comprehend its own nature. This would be like trying to see your own face without a mirror. B'reshit is not a concept about wisdom that confronts the mind like a visitor; it is the mirror of the mind itself and reflects whatever habits and tendencies the mind clings to. However, B'reshit is beyond all habits—it is the open reflectivity of the mirror that can reflect anything. It is equal before birth and after death; it is beyond change, but is the basis of all change. It is the common basis of what is known as well as that which knows it. Realization of this simultaneity is gnosis (mystical realization).

The wisdom of B'reshit continually explodes into phenomenal play. It is always arising and dissolving, beyond grasp, never static, insubstantial yet vivid. Appreciating this irrepressible wisdom in all things is the door out of the superficial, petty concerns that obscure the Divine mystery. Conversely, not appreciating it perpetuates ordinary perceptual fixation, which literally shuts the door to gnosis. This is made clear in the *Zohar*:

> B'Reshit is a key enclosing all, closing and opening. (*Haqdamat Sefer HaZohar*)

The pure Divine creative essence is referred to by the Hebrew term *Ain Sof*, which can be translated as "the infinite." The essential nature of creativity is not dependent on anything, but it is not an independent existent entity either. Ain Sof is composed of two words: Ain (without) and Sof (limitation).

No matter what phenomena arise, or do not arise, the purity and wholeness of Ain Sof is unaffected. Ain Sof cannot be diluted or subjugated, no matter how it appears to be distorted, misapprehended, or ignored. Nothing ever leaves and nothing can ever be brought in. These categories are attempts at a definition, which is impossible. All that can be said is that Ain Sof is creative and free. All concepts about Ain Sof are innately flawed, thus nothing can be known about it in the conventional sense. This is stated in the following quote from the thirteenth-century kabbalist Moshe de Leon:

> The highest crown is the pure avira (luminous space) that cannot be grasped. It is the sum of all existence, and all have wearied in their search for it. One should not ponder this "place." It is secretly named Ain Sof, for it engenders everything that is. The belt of the wise is burst by this mystery. Arouse yourself to contemplate, to

focus thought, for the Divine is the annihilation of all thoughts, uncontainable by any concept. Since no one can contain the Divine, it is called Ain (nothingness). (*Sheqel HaKodesh*)

Ain Sof is the essential unadulterated purity that arises as all things, and B'reshit is its nature. Here the esoteric dimension of language must be extremely precise. Ain Sof is pure essence, and B'reshit expresses the *nature* of that essentiality. Both aspects, the essence and its nature, are a complete unity. For example, sugar's nature is to be sweet. We know sugar through the expression of its nature in a variety of forms. No matter how the nature becomes known, it is always sweet. In any form this sweet nature expresses the essence of sugar directly, and it can be known that sugar is present.

The essence and nature of creativity are represented by the first two sefirot, called *keter* (crown) and *chochmah* (wisdom). Keter is Ain Sof's sublime essential potentiality, and chochmah is its wisdom nature. Both are included in the word B'reshit, which can be elucidated in many ways that will be described later in this book. The simplest way to understand them is to know that the two are a complete inseparable unity. This is symbolized by the letter *bet* of the word *B'reshit*. In Hebrew every letter has a numerical value, and the numerical value of *bet* is 2. This is suggested by the thirteenth-century kabbalist Isaac the Blind:

> B'reshit: The letter bet is the highest keter, and is therefore written larger than all other bets. However, the word B'reshit is in fact chochmah. In truth, then, two sefirot are encompassed within this word. (*Process of Emanation*)

To think that the essence of something can be known without the expression of its nature is deceptive. Pure essentiality cannot be communicated. It only is known through its nature. They are fundamentally the same, although they pertain to different aspects. The nature is the essence in the most dynamic sense. Creative essentiality is unknowable, but it is replete with pure cognizant potential. Its wisdom nature is the knowingness that radiates as all things, constantly beginning as each ungraspable moment.

Since the essential nature of creativity is the basis of all phenomena, nothing can be considered essentially impure or unimportant. Faith that every minute detail of life *is* this mystery radically transforms the way that life is engaged. The path to gnosis neither excludes nor reifies anything, but leaves phenomena as a brilliant open question that cannot be apprehended by self-identified beings. This unfathomability is suggested by the imagery of the following passage from an anonymously written thirteenth-century text:

> The light that is darkened from illuminating is hidden and impossible to know. Accordingly, it is called darkening darkness, not because it resembles murk, but because no creature can look at it. Even the angels seated in the front row of the kingdom of heaven lack the power to look at it. It is like a human who cannot look at the eye of the harsh sun. However, all lights emerge from it, therefore it is only called darkening darkness because it is exalted, hidden, and concealed from perception. (*The Fountain of Chochmah*)

2

BLUEPRINT OF
THE CREATIVE PROCESS

Commentary on the
First Chapter of Genesis

With-beginningness Elohim created the heavens and the earth.
(Gen. 1:1)

The first chapter of Genesis uses the Divine Name *Elohim* to designate creative power. This name is used thirty-two times in the chapter, which kabbalists associate with the "thirty-two paths of wisdom" that constitute the Tree of Life. This consists of the twenty-two letters of the Hebrew alphabet that are set into the structure of the ten sefirot. Together, the thirty-two paths constitute a perfect unity, which "speaks" the display of all phenomena. This is the heart of creativity. The gematria (numerical value) of the word for "heart" (*Lev*) is 32 (*lamed* [30] + *bet* [2] = 32). Therefore, through the name Elohim, Genesis 1 reveals the heart of the creative process.

Naming the Divine has profound implications. Exoterically, naming the Divine puts a label on a "first cause" of creative activity, which itself is causeless. It reifies this cause and renders it a substantial concept to be grasped at. If this tendency is transcended, then the role of a Divine Name can serve much more subtle functions.

The nature of creativity is unnameable. It cannot be limited to language or concepts in any conventional sense. This leaves the role of a Divine Name free to serve an investigation of how creativity functions. In kabbalah Holy names are highly complex esoteric formulas, which are deconstructed to articulate the most profound aspects of creative wisdom. Throughout this commentary, number and letter correspondences will be used to probe and elucidate many names and words. However, no esoteric excavation can be effective if what is being sought is not clear from the outset.

The name *Elohim* is associated with space, which is the womb in which the seed of B'reshit is sown. Despite this seemingly dualistic language, space is a simple unity. It is the great equalizer of phenomena. From the conventional perspective it seems that there are two aspects of space. These are the so-called absolute and relative aspects of space that some esotericists cite as categories to divide between essentiality and function. Absolute or "basic" space is the pure empty aspect of space beyond fixed qualities. "Relative" space is its ever-changing performance, contextualizing the infinite qualities that beings perceive. These artificial distinctions appear separately to human logic, but they are actually inseparable. The true nature of space is unity beyond any composite or division.

All space is really "basic" space. It is totally open, free, and pristine. However, it poses a paradox. It presents infinite contrasts and variations by appearing as phenomena. Space continually contextualizes to become all things, but cannot be contained by any of its contexts. It is a mystery that is both open and appearing. The paradox of space is illustrated vividly by the mind. The mind's expanse is an open empty potentiality, but it arises as an infinity of thoughts and perceptions. The undifferentiated space of the mind and the differentiated display of its constructs are the same cognizant space. The mind's constructs arise and dissolve, but mind itself remains untouched. This is because in the ultimate sense, space and mind are equally Ain Sof.

The pregnant vastness of space is primordial. It was not born and it will not die. It is not real and it is not unreal. It does not change, although it appears as constant change. How can it change? What is there to change? Space is only open adaptability. All measurements and calculations are equal in space. No matter what is contextualized, no matter how a thing appears "in" space, the essence of that thing is fundamentally just space as well. The play of space manifests through expansive and contractive tendencies that are like breathing. Contraction withholds and expansion gives, but nothing comes *from* anywhere or goes *to* anywhere. Where is there to go to or come from? There is nowhere outside of space.

Conventional perception assumes that space "closes up" when a particular object assumes boundaries. The function that allows things to appear in limited form is called *tzimtzum,* which means "contraction" or "withdrawal." When fixation on something occurs, it appears that undifferentiated space has withdrawn away from its boundaries to support a particular definition. Ordinary relative perception accepts the existence of things only because of their boundaries. This is like contemplating infinity in reverse.

A thing's definition is supported by all the things it is not. What defines the existence or non-existence of a thing always rests on comparison. All defined things are dependent. They rely on contrasts to sustain their boundaries, and therefore cannot be independent. Since no defined thing has real autonomous independence, all that is left to rely upon is the purity of Ain Sof. However, when the mind fixates on finite things it assumes to be real or unreal, great primordial space becomes obscured.

In truth, tzimtzum cannot actually restrain or divide space at all. Space cannot be changed. It only presents a vivid but insubstantial form of play. This play consists of reflections arising and dissolving. They have no independent existence; they simply echo like a hall of mirrors. If the wisdom of their playful, open disposition can be appreciated, the transcendent nature of phenomena can be glimpsed.

Ordinary perception is the belief in the reality of tzimtzum. A tzimtzum presents itself like a bottle sealed with a cork. When the bottle is sealed conventional perception assumes that there is a solid barrier between the space contained within the bottle and the space outside of the bottle. From the standpoint of tzimtzum this division seems to exist. However, from the radical view of mysticism this is only the intangible play of boundless space. It is all space "breathing." Space appears inside, space appears outside, and space appears as the bottle itself. An increasing number of physicists would even concede this point to a degree, admitting that the molecules of the bottle are nothing other than dynamically charged space, not essentially different than what is in and around it. The difference is that from the mystical view the energetically charged space is equal to the mind that perceives it.

When a thought arises, an enclosure appears to have been made. It appears sealed in a particular conceptual meaning, and the remainder of the mind's expanse seems to surround it, like external space surrounds the bottle. If perceptions are held in this manner they reduce perception to the status of ordinary objects. A good first step out of this predicament is simple questioning: Where do perceptions originate? Where do they go when they have finished performing? The answer to both questions is the expanse of the mind itself. This applies equally to "outer" sensory perceptions and "inner" thoughts.

The dynamic potentiality of space is called *Shechinah*. It is said that the Shechinah is like a pregnant woman who is continually gestating, giving birth, and nourishing her children. Divine space is called "mother" because it shares its lifeblood with its progeny like a womb. The "children" are the endless reflections that arise and dissolve from its mirrorlike nature. The Shechinah's womb has no borders or boundaries. It represents the whole of space, beyond the concept of containment and what is contained. Nothing enters or leaves mother space, because whatever is born is equal in nature to the space it arises within. The Shechinah continually nourishes her children by virtue of that nature, which is B'reshit. The life that is given, the children that are born, and the womb itself are all equal in the heart of Divine essential nature.

The walls of conceptual obscurity that conceal the pristine space of the mind are like clouds in the open sky of the Shechinah's radiance. The amazing thing is that since all phenomena are equally Shechinah, even the clouds are Shechinah as well. The image of the Shechinah manifesting as a cloud is given several times in the Bible. It is presented during the wandering in the desert as the cloud that follows and hovers around the view of the Israelites. At Mount Sinai, Moses went up and penetrated this cloud, going beyond its surface limitations. The common denominator of these literary images is that the Shechinah can both obscure and mitigate obscurity. The same basic space both conceals and reveals. This is the door that gnosis of B'reshit "opens and closes."

Faith is the great challenge to all conventional assumptions about the solidity of substance. The display of tzimtzum presents itself with ferocious intensity, but faith in the intangible wisdom play of the Shechinah nullifies the idea that anything fractures the unity of perfect space. Cultivating gnosis of the nature of phenomena builds certainty that the world is not a random series of objects for a subject to react to. This requires resistance to the most deep-set and most stubborn of our habits. Belief in a shattered universe only leads to suffering and alienation. How could it do otherwise? Its only products are existential isolation and alienation. Gnosis grows proportionately with the rejection of these assumptions.

> With-beginningness Elohim created the heavens and the earth. (Gen. 1:1)

In verse 1:1 the term "heaven" refers to the continuum of motion. It is summarized by six attributes that correspond to the six days of creation named in Genesis 1. This spectrum of energetic possibility defines the functional behavior of creativity. All modes of creativity are expressions of B'reshit. Thus it goes without saying that movement arises without separating or dividing anything. It does not come from anywhere or go to anywhere. All notions of place and time are only contextual constructs fabricated by conventional habit, which the inner symbolism of Genesis teaches us to resist.

Each of the six modes of energetic movement assumes its particular quality as a result of expansion and contraction. As mentioned earlier, this is like a reflection, or an echo, or like breathing. These processes are esoterically encoded within the name Elohim. This requires an analysis of the name's letters. It can be broken down into three parts. Elohim is spelled *alef-lamed-heh-yud-mem* (AL-H-YM). (NOTE: Hebrew is read from right to left, and thus it is in reversed order from the English. See figure 1.)

Figure 1

The first two letters of Elohim (*alef-lamed*) spell the Divine Name *AL* (pronounced "El"), which is associated with continuous expansion. The last two letters of Elohim (*yud-mem*) spell the word *YaM*, which means "ocean." This is the open expanse of space that has the innate tendency for tzimtzum. Within the ocean of space, infinite tzimtzumim appear and disappear like shadows, yet they present themselves with great power and beauty. The phenomena presented by tzimtzum are like vessels that are both filled and surrounded by "water," which is the essential nature of mind.

Water is the most common biblical symbol for fluid creativity because it is undifferentiated. When water fills a vessel it perfectly conforms and adapts to it, just like space does. Space never resists what it fills or surrounds. An ocean is also salt water. This corresponds with the alchemical meaning of salt, which typifies the quality of *contraction*. Salt extracts fluid from a substance, making it shrink. Thus in kabbalistic alchemy salt always refers to the aspect of tzimtzum.

AL and YaM represent the two "sides" of the creative equation. The expansive side is the *right* and the contractive side is the *left*. The meaning of the sides is a key to some of the most complex biblical symbolism. However, the most important aspect is the center between them. In the name Elohim this is presented as the letter *heh*. The letter *heh* symbolizes the Shechinah directly. It rests between right and left, expressing the heart (*lev* = 32) of creativity. The *heh* is the central presence by which expansion and contraction manifest. The attributes of right and left merely serve the center to arise as an ever-changing field of phenomena.

> The earth was tohu and bohu, and darkness covered the surface of the deep, and breath of Elohim hovered on the surface of the water. (Gen. 1:2)

Kabbalistically, the term *earth* refers to the display of apparitional space. This is what human beings assume to be real and substantial. Verse 1:2 begins by naming the earth as the primordial ground of creation. This is the aspect of space that can appear divided and fragmented through tzimtzum. The mention of earth follows the heaven. However, they are not involved in a cause and effect relationship. Heaven's formative motion and the earth's phenomenal display arise simultaneously as expressions of an equal nature.

Heaven and earth are interdependent aspects of the Shechinah's play. Next, verse 1:2 provides a valuable insight into the creative exchange between dynamism and space. The biblical words *tohu* and *bohu* are unique. These words have no exact English translations. They suggest the interactivity of the right and left sides in their manner of phenomenal play.

Tohu is often translated as "unformed," "inconceivable," or most commonly, "chaos." The term refers to the totality of dynamism that overwhelms conventional perception. Creative dynamism will always overpower any structure that tries to contain or understand it. Therefore, to the human mind the power of B'reshit becomes tohu. The power of tohu that overwhelms the meager human sense of order is kept in balance by the power of bohu. Bohu is the empty receptivity of space that is inherently contextual. Its contexts allow the potency of tohu to continually adapt to ever-changing needs. The word bohu itself articulates this function through its internal components. Aryeh Kaplan, the twentieth-century kabbalistic authority, states:

> Bohu is emptiness. This is the emptiness of a vessel ready to receive. The word can be read as two words: Bo Hu, which literally means "in it." (*Inner Space*)

The past-tense language of the first chapter of Genesis (the earth "was" tohu and bohu) refers to the primordial nature that transcends time. The nature of creativity is "prior" to human conception. This language offers a potent metaphor for that which is untainted by the vain human attempt at order. This is also hinted at by the divide between the states "before" and "after" the birth of the universe. This literary device distinguishes between uncontrived creativity devoid of human conceptual interference and the conventional understanding of linear time. This is analogous to the distinction between gnosis and human error. Time itself has no innate truth to it other than that which human beings impute. What we call time arises as the consequence of reference points fabricated by man. They are attempts to construct an artificial order within the mystery of motion.

The arising of events out of the "future," the passing of events into the "past," and even the experience of the "present" are all only categorically valid from the point of view of egoic conceptuality. Therefore tohu and bohu represent a primordial purity that is completely beyond time, and ungraspable by human intellectual standards. Tohu is the clear and present danger to the fragile balance of human psychological stability. The use of the word implies that chaos and entropy are implicit in the nature of things, which is true. All phenomena are impermanent and will eventually come apart. No thing is stable or eternal. This is because all phenomena, ultimately beyond existence and non-existence, are beyond birth and death. Once we understand this, then the danger of tohu's chaos can only threaten our habit of grasping at attachments. In addition to keeping tohu in balance, bohu is also at the heart of tohu's danger.

Beyond our well-mannered grasp, the disposition of the Shechinah is a wild and boundlessly fierce dynamic vastness. It projects all of the entropic tendencies that are manifested in cycles of decay and regeneration. The gnawing ache of this disturbance seeping through the haze of our composure is a given for most human beings. If the ordinary mind were to deviate even a little from its contrived mental strictures, the result might be insanity. This is how bohu reveals tohu. It is based in the deepest aspect of the mind's nature, which is at once our greatest love and our greatest fear. When the influence of tohu becomes unbalanced the mind becomes agitated, confused, and crazed. When bohu becomes dominant the mind becomes dazed and ineffective. The remedy to either imbalance is to remember the central heart space of the Shechinah. This is symbolized by the *heh* of the name *Elohim:* the central nucleus where both right and left tendencies commingle. Faith is simply a return to this unborn central unity.

The right and left aspects of the Shechinah's play reflect a father and mother's reproductive relationship. These tendencies are known as "seed and womb" in kabbalistic symbolism. It should be clear that they are not brought together as individual partners, but present a simultaneous mutuality that goes beyond any dualistic notion of autonomous gender parts.

The next section of verse 1:2 contains one of the most remarkable poetic images in the Bible. It involves the primordial tendencies hovering between intangible undifferentiation and the differentiated array of phenomena, which human beings fixate upon. Within this artificially divided scenario, an equalizing agent will emerge to embrace all possibility. This will become the central focus of much of the Genesis literature. First, read over the verse:

> The earth was tohu and bohu, and darkness covered the surface of the deep, and breath of Elohim (Ruach Elohim) hovered on the water's surface. (Gen. 1:2)

Picture the dividing line that the elements of this image imply. On one side is the original volatility of dynamic space, without any foothold for our conceptuality to grasp. On the other side is the same dynamic space, filled with worlds of cognizable phenomena. The undifferentiated side cannot be "seen" by human conceptual strategies. It is only a darkness that covers the depth of the Divine mystery. On the other side there is every conceivable form and sensation that the mind can fixate upon. Between them is the medium of exchange that equalizes them, the aspect of their central unity—"the breath of Elohim" or *Ruach Elohim*. Whatever you understand by this image, never take this or any biblical metaphor literally. Of course no such dividing line has existed at any time.

The great *tzaddikim* who have realized the mind's nature hold no difference between these states. They hold only to unity, and abide only as Ruach Elohim. Ordinary human thinking defines itself and everything else by the division implied here. Thus the state of the "hovering" is the exact point where perception deviates from gnosis. The "darkness covering the depth" has several meanings. It represents concealment itself, which divides the mind's nature from ordinary perception. Division is a habit that arises from the momentum of holding cognizance to be a subject and its projections to be objects. All habits are extensions of this central habit. Since both mind and its projections are nothing other than Ain Sof, this is the ultimate deceit. Habitual patterns are often set so deeply that they usually cannot even be noticed. This self-obscuring tendency is a darkness that covers all that is implied by the word "deep."

Another level of meaning is that primordial Divinity is the darkness. It does not conform to our notions of reality or unreality, thus we have no reference point by which it may be understood. It is not a substance or a lack of substance. However, it spontaneously exudes a presence by virtue of its nature. Since we cannot know it with the manner of knowing we are accustomed to, it remains a most fearsome and wondrous question. Facing this open question is what is implied later on in the Bible by the statement "no man can see the face of God and live." The primordial darkness is quintessentially creative. This means that its emptiness cannot be a mere hollow void. It is an emptiness replete with the resonant aspects of unbounded creativity. This is the aspect of darkness that is "full of light." When we follow the metaphor of darkness in the kabbalistic literature, it overlaps with metaphors of pure luminosity. (The image of a *darkness replete with cognizant luminosity* will be explored in depth in later sections of this commentary.) This is the most direct language that the kabbalistic tradition offers to lead us into the paradox of the Shechinah's capacity to express Ain Sof. It is the key to unlocking all of the central esoteric themes set out for us in all three chapters of Genesis.

The amazing thing about the great tzaddikim is that the darkness of the mind's nature is pure illumination for them. They see because they have surrendered completely to this darkness. The *Zohar* presents this paradox in relation to this section of Genesis:

> B'reshit, at the head of the royal potency, its engravings were engraved in the radiance on high. A spark of the lamp of darkness flashed within the concealed of the concealed from the head of Ain Sof. (*Zohar*)

The greatest Divine gift is that those who have realized the lamp of darkness move about in the world and teach us. They do not depart into an escapist fantasy. In fact they are way more functionally competent than ordinary people are. This is evident in the way that they reach others. All the tzaddikim desire is to be of benefit. This is directly related to the fact that they have nullified themselves to the lamp of darkness, and by virtue of that they have all the light in the world.

The Hebrew term *Ruach Elohim* has profound implications. The deep kabbalistic meaning of the word "ruach" extends far beyond its simplistic translation as "breath." The Ruach Elohim is the motive potency of the Divine essential nature that arises as states of being. Ruach Elohim is pure creative adaptability. It is the mode that creativity assumes as tohu and bohu enter into differentiation. The word *ruach* can mean "wind" in common usage. Wind is subtle and invisible atmosphere that moves. When wind becomes breath it acts as the mediator between the interior and exterior universes of a human being. In the kabbalistic sense, the external and internal manifestations of creative energy are set in motion by the primordial wind of the Ruach Elohim. Through its movement both heaven and earth are manifested.

Ruach Elohim is the transitional equalizer between pure potentiality and phenomenal form. However, conceiving of it as a division between one thing and another is pure fiction. In the literal structure of the biblical narrative Ruach Elohim stands between "before" and "after" creation. This point is quite important, because here we see that Ruach Elohim is the manifesting aspect of B'reshit. This is where we can come to terms with the creative nature and creative action simultaneously. This simultaneity is gnosis. It is called *daat,* which means knowledge in the gnostic sense.

In kabbalah the ruach refers to the aspect of the mind that assumes perceptual states. The ruach allows the mind's nature to move as the infinite diversity of cognition. It is the middle aspect of the five aspects of the "soul," which we will cover in detail later on. The ruach represents the spectrum of six attributes that corresponds to the heavens. It produces all feeling and thinking states. Thus both the internal and external aspects of energetic motion are rooted on a common model. This model is articulated kabbalistically as the ten sefirot, of which the ruach represents the middle six sefirot, from chesed to yesod.

In Hebrew the gematria (number letter value) of Ruach Elohim is 300. This number is the numerical value of the letter *shin*. The graphic form of the *shin* consists of three branches extending from a common root. This represents the unity of the three sides that represent creativity: center, right, and left. These are the essence, nature, and apparitional display that define the creative process. These three aspects are rooted together in the *shin* to represent a unity that performs as one Divine activity, the "breath of god," or Ruach Elohim.

The letter *shin* is associated with fire. This refers to the volatility inherent in creative expression, which paradoxically consumes and generates all the forms that appear to be static and fixed. The source of the fire is within appearances themselves. The activity of consuming nourishes and feeds it. The creative process displays its insatiable hunger, eating whatever it gives birth to in order to feed itself. The fire of the Ruach Elohim can be or do anything. Whatever is created is food for more creativity. This continually self-consuming fire articulates how Ruach Elohim cannot be fixed to any static state. It is the fire in the heart of all that lives, vigorously creating and fiercely destroying simultaneously.

The fire of Ruach Elohim is the vibrancy of the Shechinah. It is the phenomena created, the space within which it continually transforms, and the process of transformation itself. This terrifying ravenous aspect of the mother is almost never overtly mentioned in the formal literature. However, there are highly esoteric passages where it is alluded to. The most common of these is the altar of sacrifice in front of the Temple in Jerusalem. There, the fixed animal habits of human beings were brought to be consumed by fire in the form of living animals. The sacrificial offerings became literal embodiments of the defects of the mind, and surrendering them was akin to pouring one's heart out into the consuming fire of the Shechinah. There, the intention of the offerer, the habit that took the form of the offering, the recipient Shechinah, and the process of transformation itself were all unified. Thus they "ascend together" in Ain Sof and were nullified into basic space. This quote from the *Zohar* explains:

> Through the mystery of the offering, as it ascends, everything is bound together illuminating one another. Then all ascends, and thought is crowned in Ain Sof. The radiance from which supernal thought shines, of which (the mind) is totally unaware, is nothingness (Ain) itself. (*Zohar*)

The mystery of the fire sacrifice or "all burned offering" reveals the dependent relationship between the power that creates and the power that destroys. They are mutually defining and totally interdependent as expressions of that which cannot be born or die. We encounter this again here:

> Come and see: "For YHVH Elohenu is a devouring fire." This is a fire that devours fire, devouring and consuming it, for there is fire fiercer than fire. But come and see: Whoever wishes to penetrate the wisdom of holy union should contemplate a flame ascending from a glowing coal. Flame only ascends when grasped by a coarse substance. (*Zohar*)

And here:

> Their end is imbedded in their beginning, and their beginning in their end, like a flame in a burning coal. (*Sefer Yetzirah*)

The relationship between flame and coal illustrates *interdependency*, which nullifies the assumption of independent existence in relation to either part. Fire depends upon the coal so it can burn, and the coal is only a coal because fire burns it. Neither asserts itself apart from the other; therefore, neither can be proven to exist by itself, or can be called either real or unreal; they simply appear as aspects of a creative display with no solid basis. This analogy applies to the perception of phenomena in relation to Ain Sof. Ain Sof is creative by nature, but creativity cannot be so without some phenomenal expression. Furthermore, a phenomenon requires creativity so that it can appear. Thus, neither Ain Sof nor its apparitional display have independent existence. There are not "two real things" involved in the interdependence, since neither can be considered outside of the continuum from which these designations are derived. Each is the consequence of the other. Therefore, neither can be called stable; the dependence of each strips both of any autonomy.

The interdependent bond is the essence of the fire of the Shechinah. This is the fire at the heart of prayer and the yearning for ultimate realization. The tzaddik lives this fire completely. He knows that neither birth nor death have any independent existence whatsoever. He knows that to call Ain Sof "real" defies this wisdom. His daat is truly the door that goes *beyond god*. The remainder of the verses of the first chapter of Genesis articulate the six attributes that the Ruach Elohim assumes during the creative process. They are symbolized by the six days of creation in the narrative. These verses will be listed and commented upon separately.

DAY 1: CHESED

The expansive tendency of energy

(1:3) Elohim said: "Let light come into being," and light came into being. (1:4) Elohim saw that the light was good, and Elohim divided the light from the darkness. (1:5) Elohim called the light "day" and the darkness he called "night." It became evening and morning, one day. (Gen. 1:3–5)

DAY 2: GEVURAH

The contractive tendency of energy

> (1:6) Elohim said: "Let there be a space in the midst of the waters, and let it divide between waters and waters." (1:7) Elohim made the space and divided the waters, which were beneath the space from the waters, which were above the space, and it became so. (1:8) Elohim called the space "heaven." It became evening and morning, day two. (Gen. 1:7–8)

DAY 3: TIFERET

Energetic harmony

> (1:9) Elohim said: "Let the waters beneath the heaven be gathered into one place, and let dryness be seen," and it became so. (1:10) Elohim called the dryness "earth" and the gathering of waters he called "seas," and Elohim saw that it was good. (1:11) Elohim said: "Let the earth sprout grass, seed yielding herbs, and fruit trees bearing fruit of its kind with its seed within it upon the earth, and it became so. (1:12) The earth brought forth grass, herbs yielding seed of its kind, and trees bearing fruit which has in it seeds of its kind, and Elohim saw that it was good. (1:13) It became evening and morning, day three. (Gen. 1:9–13)

DAY 4: NETZACH

The expansive tendency within polar exchange

> (1:14) Elohim said: "Let there be lights in the space of the heaven to divide between the day and the night, and they will serve for omens for seasons for days and for years. (1:15) They will serve for light

in the space of the heaven to illuminate the earth," and it became so. (1:16) Elohim made the two great lights, the large to rule the day and the small to rule the night, and the stars. (1:17) Elohim set them in the space of the heaven to illuminate the earth. (1:18) To rule the day and the night, and to divide between the light and the darkness, and Elohim saw that it was good. (1:19) It became evening and morning, day four. (Gen. 1:14–19)

DAY 5: HOD

The contractive tendency within polar exchange

(1:20) Elohim said: "Let the waters teem with swarms of living creatures and let the birds fly above the earth in the open space of the heavens." (1:21) And thus Elohim created the great taninim, and every living creature that creeps with which the waters teem, of its kind, and every winged bird of its kind, and Elohim saw that it was good. (1:22) Elohim blessed them saying: "Be fruitful and multiply, fill the waters of the seas and let the birds multiply on the earth." (1:23) It became evening and morning, day five. (Gen. 1:20–23)

DAY 6: YESOD

The integration point of energy and its contexts

(1:24) Elohim said: "Let the earth bring forth living creatures, each of its kind, domesticated animals, creeping things, and beasts of the earth, each of its kind." And it became so. (1:25) And thus Elohim made the beasts of the earth, each of its kind, the animals each of its kind, and everything that creeps on the ground each of its kind. And Elohim saw that it was good. (1:26) Elohim said: "Let us make man in our image and likeness, and let him dominate the fish of the sea, the birds of the heaven, the animals, all the earth, and every creeping thing that creeps on the earth." (1:27) And thus Elohim created man in his image. In the image of Elohim he created him, male and female he created them. (1:28) Elohim blessed them, and Elohim said to them: "Be fruitful and multiply, fill the earth and subdue it, and dominate the fish of the sea, the birds of the heaven, and every creeping thing that moves upon the earth." (1:29) Elohim said: "Behold I have given you all seed-bearing herbs that are on the surface of the earth, and every tree that has seed-bearing fruit, to you it shall be for food. (1:30) And for every animal of the earth, for every bird of the heaven, and for everything that creeps on the ground in which there is a living nefesh, all herbs shall be their food." And it became so. (1:31) Elohim saw all that he had made and behold it was very good. It was evening and morning, day six. (Gen. 1:24–31)

The commentary on the six days requires an understanding of how the ten sefirot relate to each other independently. Each sefirah must be examined individually, which we will do in the context of the biblical narrative. The following diagram (figure 2) places the sefirot in their proper order on the right, left, and center with their corresponding days. In figure 2, binah and malkut represent *open creative space* by being suspended freely in the layout, as space itself is. The inner meaning of this will become clearer as the text progresses. This feature will unfold as one of the most profound and unique aspects of this commentary.

The ten sefirot articulate the creative array inherent in the essential Divine Name: *YHVH*. Its four letters correspond to four interdependent modes of expression that make up the unity of the creative process. The next diagram (figure 3) illustrates how the sefirot arise naturally through these four interdependent modes, expressed in unison. They are represented by four intersecting circles, each representing one of the four letters of the name YHVH.

The ten sefirot are not a representation of a linear stepped-down hierarchy, which begins at keter and concludes at malkut, contrary to popular misconception. They present Ain Sof as a unified interdependent whole with ten interactive functions. The sefirot arise together as the four letters of the Divine Name express its creative harmony. This harmonization is depicted graphically as four circles that interpenetrate one another from midpoint to periphery, as can be seen in figure 3. The "heart" of each circle is directly expressed as the outer "skin" of the next, as a single simultaneous gesture that transcends origin and cessation. If this construct is viewed beyond fixation to a linear progression, it illustrates a continuous simultaneity in which the sefirot and the four dimensions support each other interdependently.

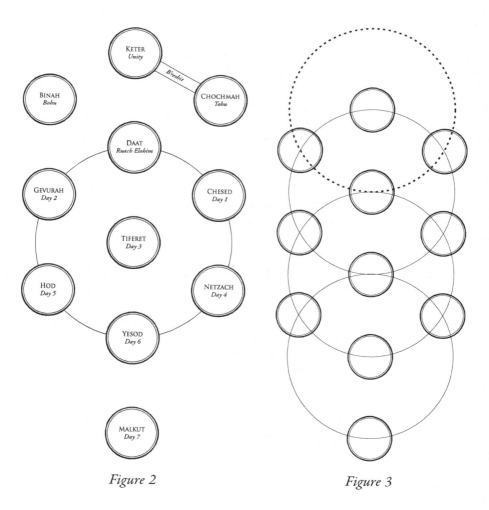

Figure 2   *Figure 3*

The construct of interpenetrating circles expressing the geometric harmony of the sefirot has appeared several times over the centuries. An early example of this, from 1682, illustrates the work of the visionary Jacob Boehme. Another can be found in a German Rosicrucian text *Geheime Figuren der Rosenkreuzer* (circa 1785). This was probably derived from exposure to Jewish sources; however, the Rosicrucian application is extensive and contains an entire system of its own. Diagrams based on these are found in several twentieth-century sources such as the works of Dr. Paul Case and Warren Kenton.

Each of the four letters of YHVH represents a dimension of the primordial unity of Ain Sof. These four dimensions are complete realms in themselves, which kabbalists refer to as the *four worlds*. Contrary to common misconception, the four worlds do not divide higher states of purity from lower states of impurity. This view, based on divisive conceptuality, belongs exclusively to the context of theistic religion.

The Divine Name is a perfectly unified continuum. Its component parts are only reference points fabricated by conceptuality to serve as tools for its understanding. However, despite its inherent unity, there is still an obvious variation in phenomenal function, which is endemic to its worlds. Herein lies the basic paradox: unity is not contradicted by diversity. Taking this as the starting point will allow the study of the sefirot to transform what may appear to be tangible qualities into intangible wisdom aspects.

The upper three sefirot (keter, chochmah, and *binah*) are referred to by the acronym *KaChaB*. These are the primordial models of interactive creative potentiality. Keter is the unborn essence of substanceless unity. Chochmah is its unceasing dynamic nature. Binah is the basic space that contextualizes its phenomenal display. All three together represent the unified matrix of possibility, which is creativity itself.

Certain older schools of kabbalah hold that there is no *essential* distinction between keter and Ain Sof. This is the view put forth in this commentary. Later schools of kabbalah take this as heresy on theistic grounds, as they hold that there must always be some aspect of distance between emanator and emanation (see Ramak). If this stance is rejected, it might be asked why there is a designation for keter in the first place. Since keter literally means "crown," it sets unity at the "head" of all creative function. Keter is a reminder that Ain Sof is always silently implicit, and asserts unchangeable purity as continual change. The crown seals the sefirot with the royal view beyond extremes. It is the guiding rule, which posits that all the sefirot (and all phenomena) are equal in nature, even though differences in function arise continually. Keter extends this paradox as a head does its body. It reminds us that Ain Sof and its functions are only divided conceptually. As such, the relationship between Ain Sof and keter summarizes the central paradox of the creative process. We return to the heart of this paradox by faith, which is adherence to a unity that cannot be shattered by the diversity of phenomena.

Later kabbalistic schools hold that keter is a "step below" Ain Sof and believe that it operates as an agent on behalf of unrepresentable, unspeakable mystery. This split is the beginning of many complex divisions within keter itself, which is the basis of a cosmological system that attempts to explain the origin of "evil." This cosmic development is referred to as the "shattering of the vessels." It begins with the supernal sefirot breaking apart and "falling" to form the lower worlds, which present themselves in fragments as a result of the primordial shattering. The later schools believe that human beings piece the fragments of Holiness back together and elevate them through Divine service. Most spiritual seekers will be ill served by these ideas. It is far better to uphold that nothing has ever been divided from anything else. Radical adherence to unity can and should be maintained, as the alternative is a dalliance with a dualistic view based on a war between the forces of unity and chaos.

Divine essence and its nature cannot be separated, like sugar and its sweetness or water and its wetness. Thus keter and chochmah are both considered aspects of the first letter of the Divine Name: the *yud* of YHVH. The *yud* is graphically divided into two parts: the upper tip, which represents keter, and the swelling body that extends the tip, which represents chochmah. The apex point of the *yud* symbolizes an "ideal" or "absolute" point, which is a perfect dimensionless unity. An absolute point is indivisible, thus it cannot be reduced to relative dualistic contrasts. All of space, and all the coordinates and relationships that are possible within it, are equal from the perspective of an absolute point.

In the Talmud, the wise men of Athens (representing linear rational thought) asked the rabbis: "Where is the center of the universe?" A rabbi pointed up with his finger at random and said: "here." This implies that the central heart point is omnipresent, because the point of beginningness abides everywhere equally; therefore, it must also be "here." Then the Athenians asked the Rabbis: "How do you know this?" They responded: "Bring a rope and we'll measure." The story implies that all relationships between points become viable through the open possibility that the absolute point of keter presents. Measurement emerges from its undifferentiated "beginningness." Since this possibility is unfixed and omnipresent, all relationships between relative points can be fabricated equally. No absolute logistical center can be pinpointed in any specific location, so measurement begins wherever the concept of its inception arises. This is how conceptual divisions arise in the minds of human beings. Open possibility is the essential nature of the mind, but fixation on concepts depends on fabricated measurement arising within it. Since the "beginning" of this process is all-pervasive in the mind, the conceptual "measuring rope" the Athenians asked for is a literal afterthought that can easily manifest whenever it is called upon.

Ain Sof can only be expressed through the projection of chochmah, which is its own radiant nature. Chochmah is the "shining forth" of the open potentiality of keter, thus it is referred to as the light (*aur*) of Ain Sof. This radiant nature is the life inherent within all of space and all phenomena. This is represented by the extension of the apex point into the *yud's* body.

In sacred geometry, chochmah is represented by an endless line that radiates the primordial point of keter anywhere and everywhere. This is the luminosity of B'reshit that continuously makes itself available without limitation. It is replete with the capacity to *become*. The point and its line represent an undifferentiated unity beyond beginning and ending. Neither can be located, but both are implicit in all locations. They are the infinite basis of every finite entity. This is the mystical basis of the "rope" brought out by the rabbis in response to the Athenians. It is the gnostic basis of all conventionally measured or known things.

The translation of chochmah is "wisdom." This is the wisdom of pure cognizance, the mind's unborn nature. This cognizant lucency is the raw knowingness that makes all of the mind's phenomena possible. From a relative point of view, phenomena are divided between internal and external manifestations. These and all divisions are arbitrary from the perspective of wisdom. Chochmah's illumination is so far beyond subject-object fixated cognition that it is referred to as "darkness" in mystical literature. This is because its light cannot be reduced to substantial or tangible terms. It does not arise from somewhere to shine to somewhere else. It is illumination beyond any measurable origin or destination.

The *yud* is the graphic basis of all Hebrew letters. The continuity between the keter-tip and chochmah-body is evident as the point in the upper left corner of each letter, before it morphs into its specific shape. In this sense, all Hebrew letters are considered elaborations of the *yud*. This indicates the innate presence of essential wisdom in the heart of all of speech. Kabbalistically, the creative generation of phenomena is referred to as "Divine speech." This implies that all phenomena are an expression of the light of Ain Sof. All phenomena "spoken into being" by Elohim reflect this essential nature, which is B'reshit. This applies to every possible letter combination and the infinite variation they project. Thus B'reshit (keter-chochmah) is the central manifesting power of creativity found in all things. See figure 4 on page 42.

Figure 4

The *yud* also has a lower taper, which is its third graphic element. This is where the flow of supernal light enters into the ocean of binah. The three aspects (apex, body, and lower taper) are suggested in the following quote by the terms "root," "stream" and "droplet":

> Yud is a fountain: its roots are rooted and its streams are connected and its droplets are based in the wholeness of the circle. (*The Fountain of Chochmah*)

The triad KaChaB (keter, chochmah, binah) can be understood in the manner of a circle. A circle is constructed through the interaction of three parts: center point, radial line, and periphery. These correspond to keter, chochmah, and binah, respectively. The center point represents the essential potency that only assumes a fixed position relative to a set of boundaries. It extends itself as a line, which can stop at an infinite range of secondary points. It can manifest an entire world in which infinite internal relationships can appear. This is made possible by *envelopment,* which is the consequence of the line rotating in a 360-degree arc around its center point. This circumscribes both line and center within a circular periphery.

When the line stops, it assumes measured length. Then it is taken for a segment and its radiant nature becomes obscured, and it appears "closed." Therefore a distinction can be made between the line's true nature and the appearance of its relative function. The same is true of the circle's periphery, which is the total "self-envelopment" of the line. The relative appearance of the periphery suggests a boundary, but its nature is as open as the line is. It manifests anywhere radiance arises, and represents the contextual expanse of the line's infinite capacity for "play."

✳

From the highest view, the circle represents open space contextualizing whatever luminosity asserts. If this is honored, the point represents the heart of creativity, the line is its radiant nature, and the periphery is all-encompassing space. All three are of equal value and are a complete unity. However, if only measurement is honored, then the point represents logistical position, the line is a measuring tool, and the periphery is a mere boundary. All three are then fixated upon as "objects," when a view based on measurement freezes their open creative nature. This equates measurement with fixation. It is analogous to conceptuality stopping the mind with the assumption that something "exists." This obscures the open apparitional possibility of space and its light. This happens wherever the mind fixates on phenomena. The circle becomes a symbol of limitation if its nature is obscured and forgotten. When this occurs only a superficial "shell" (*klipah*) remains. However, if all three aspects express open dynamic creativity, the circle is a symbol of wholeness and freedom. To this view, apparitional enclosures come and go, but the Divine nature that makes them possible is honored.

Binah is primordial space, replete with unborn essentiality and its luminous nature. Space is simply the open potential for phenomena. It does not change in essence, but always changes in appearance. It allows infinite worlds to be possible, just like infinite circles can be constructed anywhere from the omnipresent point and the radiance of its line. As such, binah is the culminating expression of the supernal triad (KaChaB), which is a perfect creative unity.

Binah corresponds to the *upper heh* of YHVH. As mentioned earlier, every Hebrew letter derives its form from the *yud*. The *yud* is graphically located in the *heh's* upper horizontal, which is like a long horizontal *yud*. However, *heh* relates to *yud* in a more intimate manner, which is like a pregnant womb to its impregnating seed. The *heh* represents the primordial capacity to reflect infinite tzimtzumim. This capacity to contextualize and display phenomena is made possible by the innate presence of its superabundant wisdom light, which is *yud*.

Their simultaneity is demonstrated by a classic esoteric formula found in the *Zohar,* where all Hebrew letters can be spelled out as words. This is called the "letter name" of the letter. The letter name of *yud* is spelled: *yud-vav-dalet* (YVD). When graphically combined, the *dalet* and *vav* of the *yud's* letter name create the graphic form of the *heh*. It implies that the *heh* is already in the *yud*, as all of space and its contexts are primordially possible within the light of Ain Sof. The next *Zohar* quote and diagram prove this (figure 5).

Figure 5

From yud arise male and female: vav and dalet. Yud is male, heh is female. (*Sifra Dtzniuta*)

The presence of the *heh* within the *yud's* letter name seems to suggest that space arises *from* light; however, this is not so. The relationship only proves that luminosity and space share a common original nature. They are completely co-emergent and simultaneous, and equally express a unity beyond sequential order. The relationship of luminosity and space is referred to in kabbalah in reproductive terms—chochmah is called *father* (the seed) and binah is *mother* (the womb). The paradox is that the womb is present within the seed, which ultimately impregnates it. Kabbalistically, space is continually pregnant. Thus it is obvious that their simultaneity is beyond the conceptual structure of sequential order and time. This reproductive simultaneity expresses the truth about the creative nature, which is beyond dualistic contrasts. As the seed fertilizes its own womb a common essential unity is evident. This is keter, which is the unity of Ain Sof inherent in the reproductive play of chochmah and binah.

The following quotation from the *Zohar* refers to the co-emergent simultaneity of luminosity and space as "split but not split." This passage is written from the perspective of keter—the heart point beyond time and location. It refers to a paradox that expresses both variation and wholeness without any contradiction. This is the essential mystery of creativity: it is simultaneously diverse and unified, beyond all extremes. Its dynamism is symbolized by what the quotation calls an "impact of splitting" that "cannot be known." The *Zohar* states:

> Deep within the lamp gushed a flow splaying color below, concealed within the concealed of the mystery of Ain Sof. It split but did not split the luminosity of its space, and could not be known, until under the impact of splitting a single concealed supernal point shined. Beyond the point nothing is known, so it is called B'reshit. (*Zohar*)

The co-emergent equality of the father and mother is nullified to Ain Sof. They have no separate identity other than the perpetuation of unborn creativity. This is what faith, as described here, reminds us of: nothing has any separate independent existence; all appears vividly and wondrously. This magical disposition can be relied upon to nullify anything that is mistakenly thought to be separate. It can dissolve the fiction of any temporal or logistical fixation in the midst of activity. To nullify fixation does not mean that anything vanishes or escapes; it simply implies cutting the root of the mind's attachment. When human beings aspire to this stance, primordial creativity is given a chance to realize its limitless splendor.

The role of keter (which typifies nullification and unity) is illustrated by two important names used in the *Zohar*. The names are *Atika Kadisha,* which means "Holy Ancient One," and *Atik Yomin,* which means "Ancient of Days." These names allude to the transcendence of time and the relative circumstances of motion. Fabricating a temporal framework assures the superficial perception of events, like perceiving a circle's parts based only on measurement. What is primordially "ancient" goes beyond this and all frameworks that portend to structure anything. Keter is the "original" unity of luminosity and space, which is beyond the limitation of any circumstantial enclosure. Its wisdom is reflected in the following *Zohar* quotation from the *Idra Rabba* section:

> Chochmah includes everything, and emerges and shines from Atika Kadisha as male and female. It survives only by another aspect of male and female. As chochmah expanded it produced binah from itself. Chochmah and binah are weighed as equal measure. Chochmah is a father to all fathers. (*Idra Rabba*)

Primordial wisdom is called the "father to all fathers." This seed of creativity includes every possibility, including the possibility of open space in which phenomena are gestated and born. This is "chochmah producing binah from itself." There is a profound gematria that sheds light on chochmah's nature. As mentioned above, the word for "light" in Hebrew is *aur,* which has a numerical value of 207 (AVR: A [1] + V [6] + R [200] = 207). This numerical value is shared with the words *Ain Sof,* and also with the word that typifies its mystery: *raz* ("secret"). We can conclude from this gematria that the concealed secret essence of Ain Sof is absolutely equal with the creative expression of its light. This is the wisdom of Atika Kadisha, which is known in the paradox of simultaneity, both vivid and without independent existence.

The light of Ain Sof is the "heart" of the Shechinah's pregnancy. It is the "central" nature of all things, which is equal to keter. This is the basis of the Shechinah's capacity to gestate, give birth, and nourish all phenomena. This is presented in the following thirteenth-century passage. Note that the Shechinah is positioned at the "head," which is a reference to keter:

She is in the middle, and encompasses, and is positioned at the head. She suckles power for all, and is sustained with all. All are drawn and emerge from her. (*The Fountain of Chochmah*)

The pregnancy of the Shechinah gives birth to gnosis and fixation equally, without either one dividing its essential nature. All phenomena assert this paradox. The phenomenal display of Ain Sof is continuous, insubstantial, and vividly wondrous; however, within its perfect unity "imperfection" is presented. From the view of "original purity," even the word *impurity* is pure. However, from the ordinary point of view of fixation on subjects and objects, impurity and purity are opposites in continual conflict.

The Shechinah is the original space of all views. Its pristine pregnant potentiality is binah, but the assumption of its phenomenal array of contexts constitutes the sefirah *malkut*. Malkut is represented by the *final heh* of YHVH. What is the difference between binah and malkut? Space does not change or divide. The difference between them only reveals human fixation. From the view of original purity they are equal in the essential nature of space, but from the view of conventional perception malkut is set apart by defining characteristics. From this point of view malkut represents a "broken" universe of parts in which differences and divisions appear to be real.

Between binah and malkut the attributes of the six days, which define creative movement, assume their characteristics. Motion defines energy, time, and perception. Kabbalistically, the six aspects are "in" the space of Shechinah, which binah and malkut present. The main question is: What is the disparity between malkut and binah?

The *Zohar* quotation (on page 46) stated chochmah emerges from Atika Kadisha as male and female and survives by another aspect of male and female. The usual interpretation of this passage articulates how manifestation is asserted through keter. Phenomena are expressed as a dance of luminosity and space, which is extended as an infinite chain of interactive contrasts. Contrasts arise within contrasts, and on and on, like a hall of mirrors. These are the reflections that arise as supernal space displays its mirrorlike nature.

Between malkut and binah all perceptual habits are formed. These habits are imputed upon the space of malkut, and thus its appearance is taken to be "reality." The habit of fixation renders its original purity opaque, and spacious luminosity becomes locked within myriad reflected appearances. Their phenomena become reified as the mind tries to covet and grasp them. This renders binah and malkut seemingly separate, and perpetuates their disparity.

Kabbalists refer to binah and malkut as the *upper and lower aspects of the Shechinah.* The upper water represents basic space, the union of womb and seed, which never changes. The lower aspect reflects infinitely changing and adapting conditions that reflect the mind's habits. Both fixation as well as clear gnosis can be reflected in malkut's space. If the former dominates, then phenomena are reduced to the status of fragmented objects. If the latter dominates, then unity prevails; binah and malkut cease to be divided.

Binah is called the "male" water because it is unified with the primordial seed and is indivisible. Malkut is called "female" because it manifests according to change, and either blocks or invites in the "male" aspect. These terms are only provisional, as the two *heh*s usually represent a basic femininity. They are only called male and female to articulate the manner in which the illusion of their separation is manufactured.

The ten sefirot as a whole are also divided according to gender. There are five males called *chasadim* (keter, chochmah, chesed, tiferet, netzach) and five females called *dinim* (binah, gevurah, hod, yesod, malkut). This is another layer of what the previous *Zohar* quotation referred to as "survival according to another aspect of male and female." Together the five male and five female sefirot display the wholeness of *yud. Yud* has a numerical value of ten. Its complete essential nature is expressed as it unfolds its space display, like a mouth parting two lips to speak. This is precisely what happens as the creative edicts of

Genesis are uttered. Through this Holy speech creative motion arises in space, and the six sefirot between binah and malkut assume their attributes.

The *heh* has numerical value of five, and thus its two aspects represent a tenfold unity, which reflects the *yud*. Fivefold expression is called the "handprint" of the Shechinah, and the *Sefer Yetzirah* gives a formula of dual fives in the symbol of two hands that are held aloft in prayer. These two hands establish a bond, which is the sum of ten created by the two sets of five fingers. Their bond alludes to the "covenant" that unifies flawed human perception with Ain Sof. This reflects the mystery that the *Zohar* calls "splitting but not splitting." The *Sefer Yetzirah* relates the covenant to the non-dual essence of the ten sefirot. It refers to it as *belimah* (nothingness), which is a name of Ain Sof. Recognizing nothingness nullifies phenomena and the paradox of a unified multiplicity beyond extremes becomes apparent:

> Ten sefirot of Nothingness (belimah): In the number of ten fingers, five opposite five, with a singular covenant precisely in the middle. (*Sefer Yetzirah*)

The word *belimah* consists of two words: *beli* (without) and *mah* (something). It has a gematria of 87. This is the gematria of the phrase *Ani YHVH* which means "I god" or "I am god." This phrase appears at various points in the Bible, and it is a hint that explodes the myth of a concrete theistic deity. It suggests that pregnant potentiality or "nothingness" is the true basis of the sefirot, which by extension is also all creativity and gnosis.

Kabbalistically all phenomena are symbolically divisible by five. The fivefold nature of phenomena is metaphorically referred to in the *Tikkuney Zohar* as "five colors." These colors articulate how the light of Ain Sof reflects between binah and malkut. It states:

Yud is her measure. The supernal Heh is five times light. The lower
Heh is the five colors where the five lights shine. When the upper
Heh expands to shine in the lower Heh, into her five shades, imme-
diately the vav expands toward her. (*Tikkuney Zohar*)

The eighteenth-century Chassidic master Rebbe Nachman of
Breslov uses this format to articulate how the daat (knowledge) of gnosis is made possible. He states that "five things" cultivate Divine realization. These are not five separate things; they represent the fivefold
presence inherent in all things. It is the common denominator of the
Shechinah which establishes the covenant "between the hands" in all
phenomena. Rebbe Nachman states:

There is no difference between human daat and the daat of God,
other than five things. From this man's daat nourishes from God's
daat. (*Likutey Moharan*)

The daat of the "five things" is cultivated when phenomena are
engaged with the intention of honoring the Shechinah's purity. This
can be introduced by kabbalistic correspondences that represent phenomena as a series of fivefold patterns. Here are some correspondences
that illustrate this:

Five divisions of sefirot: malkut; middle six; binah; chochmah;
keter
Five aspects of mind (or "soul"): apparitional vitality (nefesh/*heh*);
thinking and feeling (ruach/*vav*); space of thought (neshamah/
heh); nature of mind (chayah/*yud*); essence (yechidah/tip of *yud*)
Five worlds: apparitional form (assiah); energy (yetzirah); axiom-
atic space (briah); luminosity (atzilut); guiding essence (keter-
Adam Kadmon)
Five elements: earth; air; fire; water; essential nature of space
Five senses: touch; taste; hearing; smell; sight.

The *Tikkuney Zohar* quotation points out that the *vav* emerges as malkut and binah are bound in relationship. The *vav* of YHVH is the unceasing motion that extends the dynamism of B'reshit into energetic patterns. Graphically a *vav* is a *yud* with its lower taper extended all the way down. This extension represents the "descent" of manifesting energy, which carries B'reshit into phenomena.

The graphic presence of the *yud* is the *vav's* "head" both literally and figuratively. This connection illustrates how energy extends its essential nature. Its adaptation as six types of motion (*vav* = 6) is articulated in the *Tikkuney Zohar:*

> B'reshit: BaRA ShYT (six are created). Who are they? Six chambers. Elohim Supernal mother is over them, for she is the seventh. Just as Supernal mother emanates six so also the manifest mother reveals six. Who are they? The heaven and the earth. (*Tikkuney Zohar*)

This ingenious quotation rearranges the letters of the word B'reshit to say "six are created." These are the six middle sefirot, called "six chambers," to illustrate how energy is contextualized by space. The term "chamber" expresses the adaptive tendency of space. Space conforms to support whatever energetic motion manifests. In this manner the six chambers of energy bind malkut and binah, space to space, and thus the *vav* joins the two *hehs* as a single continuous expression.

The key to these correspondences will be expressed in a unique construction called "the Divine Image diagram" (figure 7). It places the four letters of YHVH within the geometric harmony of the ten sefirot as introduced by the four interpenetrating circles. Having investigated the nature of the circle, it should be clear that each of the four "worlds" is an expression of the primordial creativity of KaChaB, and is of an essentially equal value.

The Divine Image diagram illustrates the central pattern inherent in all expressions of creativity. It is directly reflected in the configuration of the human body, which suggests that human beings are designed for gnostic realization. Humans are the only beings that can achieve this. The human realm rests somewhere between the dense habit of gross solidity and the freedom of the mind's nature. This "halfway" position has profound benefits. It gains a sense of immanent facticity from phenomena, and also gets the chance to expand its vividness into the spacious vastness of its ground. When these aspects of phenomenal vividness and basic space cease to be taken as separate, then gnosis awakens.

Figure 6

The model of how the four letters create the simple vertical image of a standing human form should be examined (figure 6 above). The correspondence between the letters of YHVH and the human body has several kabbalistic variations. The one employed here works in the following manner: the *yud* is the head, the upper *heh* is the axis of the shoulders and arms, the *vav* is the spine, while the axis of the hips and legs is the final *heh*. This likeness will be presented in verse 1:26 (day six) when the creation of human form is given.

The Divine Image diagram is a code that unpacks the esoteric content of Genesis 1–3. It will become clear that this is a blueprint of the creative process, which has ramifications that exceed the scope of this commentary. The diagram can be applied to all the books of the Bible, as well as to many gnostic and alchemical works. It is present in most kabbalistic works in one form or another.

The shaded spaces above the upper *heh* and below the lower *heh* (in figure 7) illustrate the *upper and lower waters*. This reveals the

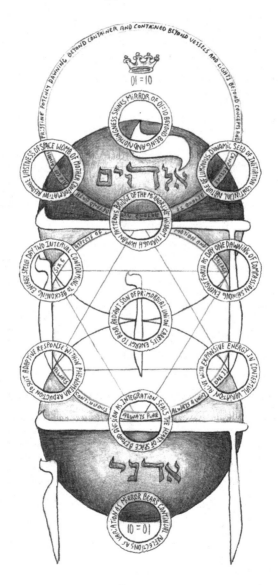

Figure 7

scope of the binah and malkut aspects of the Shechinah. Binah and malkut are the only sefirot that do not touch the four letters of YHVH directly in the diagram. They are suspended like space itself. The unity of these aspects and the ever-present danger of dualizing them is suggested by a famous mystical passage from the Talmud. When speaking metaphorically about coming into the realization of the mind's nature, Rabbi Akiva gives the following as a warning:

> When approaching the place of pure marble do not say: "water-water." As is said, "He who speaks falsely will not be sustained before my eyes." (*Chagigah*)

Repeating "water" when on the brink of realization implies that the lingering belief in dualizing extremes still persists. This is the antithesis of gnosis, which is symbolized by infinite water without division. The appearances of life always appear divided, but adherence to unity despite this apparent contradiction is the true test of faith. Thus "water-water" represents the challenge that is presented in every cognitive act. It is the true test of what the Shema proclaims.

To analyze the diagram in detail we must understand the inner symbolism of the graphic form of the letter *heh*. *Heh* is composed of three parts: a horizontal top and two side "legs." The right leg connects directly to the horizontal top and the left is detached or segmented. The horizontal top of the letter is very important. It poses an artificial division between the undifferentiated space above the letter and the bounded space below it, between the letter's "legs." This distinction is a microcosm of the upper and lower waters within a single *heh*. Above is its binah aspect and below is its malkut aspect. However, as known, both are completely equal in the paradox of "water-water."

The space below the horizontal, within the letter's legs, is where endless phenomenal reflections manifest. The tendencies of the right and left sides exert their influence there. The space above cannot be limited by any influence or condition. Thus the graphic device of the horizontal indicates tzimtzum, which is the heart of the creative paradox. Tzimtzum appears to divide appearances and project that sense of division into infinite echoes that reflect inside space. As is known, this creative play adjusts to the manner in which it is perceived. The play of tzimtzum never becomes real or unreal except in the perception of beings. Tzimtzum is an open invitation to manifest the mind's habits. In the illustration below, the echoes of tzimtzum are depicted within the *heh* of the name Elohim. It echoes seven times (representing the lower seven sefirot). Set vertically in relation to it is the name of chochmah: *Yah* (*yud-heh*). This placement allows the *yud* of Yah to represent supernal expanse above the horizontal (figure 8).

Figure 8

A person perceives completely unique phenomena in each moment because tzimtzum is always unique. Phenomena are a product of the mind, and cognition itself is a constant state of uniqueness. Tzimtzum is unceasingly creative and pervasively adjustable to the infinite range of the human mind. This is the key to the symbolism of the *heh*. Its horizontal appears to be a dividing line, but the Shechinah is indivisible. The horizontal projects the shadow of the perceptual habits of beings throughout space. It is like the periphery of a circle, which waits to emerge to enclose and conceal basic space, wherever it is asked to do so. Space is replete with the capacity to seal itself up, if invited by perceptual habit. Because the three supernal sefirot that create circles are all pervasive, the cusp of the Shechinah's womb can contract wherever humans limit the scope of their minds.

The spaces above and below a *heh's* horizontal are interdependent. Above is pure boundless creativity, and below continually adapting phenomena are manifested. Each depends on the other "like a flame and a burning coal." There can be no creativity without the display of phenomena. How could it be called creative without it? There cannot be phenomena without creativity. On what basis would it arise? Therefore neither exists independently; each depends on the other for its purpose and distinctiveness. They are a creative unity, and are only separated in artificial conceptual terms.

In the Divine Image diagram the upper *heh's* horizontal falls at the sefirah of daat. Daat corresponds with the Ruach Elohim, which marks the transition between the three supernal sefirot and the lower seven sefirot. Kabbalistically this differentiates the "head" from the "body." However, it is not so easy. The nature of the Ruach Elohim is equal in both of them. This is the heart of the paradox of the "Ruach Elohim that hovered upon the water's surface." The undifferentiated creativity above and its differentiated attributes below are not separate in any way. Yet it cannot be denied that the appearance of separation presents itself. The cure for the mind's habit of reification and division is direct immersion in this central paradox. The Ruach Elohim is raw creativity that arises as seemingly diverse phenomena. This Holy paradox is the nature of the Shechinah.

The lower *heh* also manifests interdependency. Energy cannot move without the context of space to move in, and space cannot act contextually without motion manifesting within it. All of this happens below the upper *heh*'s horizontal. In the Divine Image diagram the lower *heh*'s own horizontal falls on yesod, at the midpoint between heaven (middle six) and earth (malkut). At yesod, motion and space may or may not be recognized as a unity. When these states are integrated below, the wholeness of daat is realized, just as it is above. However, dualistic habit patterns in yesod can also "freeze" perception. This happens as consciousness grasps at the insubstantial reflections of malkut, which creates barriers and obstructions between yesod's upper and lower aspects. This "thickens" yesod, blocking the assimilation of daat into the "body" of the tree.

The *heh*'s horizontal is a "window" through which phenomena are seen. The letter *heh* represents vision itself. Every Hebrew letter has a kabbalistic symbol to which it corresponds, and the attribution for the *heh* is a window. This window does not look "into" or "out from" anything, it is cognizant space itself, the essence of the Shechinah. Remembering this will nullify belief in divisive subjects and objects. It reminds us of the interdependent creativity beyond beginnings and endings. It reminds us to avoid the error of "water-water," so the limitless display of visionary variation can be appreciated without attachment. Spiritual breakthroughs happen when the window of vision is purified and made clear. The cultivation of this clarity is daat, which means "knowledge" (in the mystical sense). When yesod opens its obstructing tendencies, daat is pervasive in the lower seven sefirot. Daat is the primordial coalescence of the father's seed with the mother's womb. It is the "dew" of the water of B'reshit, which becomes the six days, which is the *vav* that unifies the two *heh*s. The *vav*'s sixfold motion is called the "son" of the father and mother. The supernal parents are also known as the "king and queen." When malkut's apparitional space is held as equal to the basic space of binah, then the "son" inherits his parents' kingdom. This opens the visionary scope of the sefirot, and allows each act of cognition to display its inherent purity. This is expanded in this *Zohar* quotation:

Yud and heh join and conceive and produce a son. Thus binah is BeN YaH. This is perfection; both merge with the son between them, a complete perfection. (*Idra Rabba*)

The name *binah* is spelled *bet-yud-nun-heh* (*BYNH*). These letters when rearranged spell *BeN YaH* which means "son of Yah." *Yah* is the Divine Name of chochmah the father. The name is spelled *yud-heh* (*YH*), which is remarkable because these two letters also refer to chochmah and binah respectively. This indicates the simultaneity and co-emergence of seed and womb. This hidden connection makes it clear that binah is mother of creative motion (son), and is inseparable from its essential nature (father). Whatever manifests through the window of the Shechinah can be understood as "son of Yah," the direct extension of the mind's sublime nature. This illustrates that creative motion is only the extension of chochmah's dynamism, and space is inseparably central to all.

The son manifests his motion through the expansive and contractive tendencies of energy. This is represented in the Divine Image diagram by the two legs of the upper *heh*, which straddle either side of the *vav*. The right leg connects directly to the *heh's* horizontal, illustrating continuous and ceaseless expansion. The left leg is detached, illustrating the intervals that differentiate phenomena. The *yud* is unified with the upper water of the diagram, which illustrates the essential nature of the YaM, the supernal wisdom-ocean. This ocean is binah, whose name conceals the link between father (YaH) and son (BeN). Thus the creative energy of the six days is basic space in motion, which extends primordial dynamism into play. Next comes a kabbalistic analysis of each of the six days. Before this, consider the illustration (figure 9) of the crowning of the son (vav = 6) by the supernal mother and father from the alchemical classic *Philosophia Reformata* (Mylius, 1622).

Figure 9
(Johann Daniel Mylius, Philosophia Reformata, *1622)*

DAY I

Elohim said: "Let light come into being," and light came into being.
(Gen. 1:3)

The light of the first day corresponds to the sefirah of chesed, whose attributes are boundless love and energetic expansion. This light represents energy in the most general sense. It extends directly without interruption from the Ruach Elohim into the "body" of the tree through the motion of the six sefirot of the heavens, which express their attributes between the upper and lower waters.

The movement of the heavens brings up an important question: If the upper and lower waters are both aspects of basic space, where is the space between them? Where is the "place" in which it moves? It should always be remembered that space is not "anywhere" in a substantial sense. The notion of "place" is only a by-product of conceptual measurement. Space itself is free, beyond all place and time. However, from a diagrammatic point of view, the light of chesed shines into manifestation from the Ruach Elohim at the sefirah of daat. This provisional concept helps the intellect understand the precise details of the creative process, but the definitive meaning is always unity. Space and light both "above" and "below" are equally Ruach Elohim, which is the living daat of the Shechinah.

Recalling the view of radical unity corrects the mistaken belief that the six days literally emerge "from" the Ruach Elohim. There is nowhere to go to or come from. This is the disadvantage of diagrammatical thinking. Esoteric language and visual representations must never be taken literally, and spatial literality should never be assumed. The primordial light of chochmah and the manifest light of chesed are profoundly different in a conceptual sense. Diagrammatically they are placed "before" and "after" creation, which occurs at daat. The light of chochmah is inexpressible, and beyond all temporality; therefore, this (or any designation) cannot apply. This is the subject of the following thirteenth-century quotation from the School of Azriel of Gerona:

> Primordial chochmah is the light of life, pure and refined like gold sealed in the radiance of the splendorous expanse of the exalted which is Ain (nothingness). It is devoid of conceptualization. (*Contemplation—Thirteen Powers*)

The wisdom-light of chochmah becomes known in a conventional sense through the light of chesed. Chesed extends pure primordial potentiality as all phenomena. It is simply a subset of chochmah's power. Their common nature is expressed in the *Zohar*:

> "... and Light came into being ..." This is a light that already was. This light is a concealed mystery, an expansion expanding, burst-

ing from the mysterious secret of hidden supernal luminous space. (*Zohar*)

The energy of chesed is pure compassion in action. Chesed is compassionate for no other reason than it displays the Divine essential nature. From the gnostic perspective, every aspect of creation is fundamentally compassionate because everything shares this common nature. However, from the conventional human perspective, this is not the case. Suffering, loss, and death characterize ordinary perception, even though the nature of these and all qualities are equal in the nature of B'reshit. Even the fearsome wrath of the Divine is Holiness. This is the difficult aspect of the paradox: Divine compassion does not conform to human likes and dislikes, our personal welfare, or even our "life" or "death." Divine compassion cannot be understood by the rational intellect at all. This is stated by Rebbe Nachman:

> The entire creation was created, from the inception of atzilut all the way to the center point of the corporeal world, in order to display Divine compassion. (*Likutey Moharan*)

The compassion Rebbe Nachman refers to includes all the harsh as well as all the joyful aspects of life. The light of chesed has no specific form. It is manifested undifferentiatedly and becomes all worlds and all activities. Chesed is associated with mercy and goodness, but the true meaning of this has to be understood in a scope greater than human psychological tastes. True mercy is not just "getting what we want." Chesed expands life's variations, regardless of what may arise. This expansivity drives all movement; it makes things "go." It is the direct extension of chochmah within manifestation.

Chochmah and chesed are diagrammatically situated above and below the horizontal of the upper *heh* on the right side. This distinction has monumental implications. Cognitive obscurations only arise below the horizontal. The light of chesed manifests all conventional thoughts and feelings "between the waters." In contrast, chochmah's wisdom light is beyond conventional comprehension, so it is called "unmanifest" light in certain texts.

Gnosis of chochmah must be realized directly. In contrast, chesed's light can be experienced even while it is distorted beyond recognition. Chesed is pure compassion, but the light of manifestation often reveals a horror show. This produces confusion, and causes most people to live in alienation and fear. The mind's distortions block the direct recognition of chochmah. However, when wisdom (as gnosis) is cultivated, the radiance of chesed can be recognized as the projection of chochmah's continuum, and all phenomena become part of that continuum. This manifests boundless Divine compassion. When this is not cultivated then wisdom will seem irretrievably lost. Losing touch with supernal wisdom is the defining characteristic of all conventional thought and perception.

Deep faith in the basic goodness of manifestation can allow wisdom to sparkle through conventional fixation in the form of "gnostic intuitions." Even while trapped in the reified tzimtzum of daily life, one can still intuit that vastness and luminosity are actually the true nature of all things. This directly opposes the tendency that dominates the habits of the ordinary mind. This is what the kabbalistic literature refers to as the "mitigation" of the influence of tzimtzum. When its influence is relaxed, chesed emerges to invite the mind to follow into its pure wisdom source. This opens the door into the compassionate nature of energy. Chesed's compassion allows glimpses of chochmah, but few realize this in the midst of the morass of reflections that cloud the ordinary mind.

The internal structure of the statement: "Let there be light, and light came into being" reveals profound kabbalistic wisdom. Concealed in this statement is a multifaceted vision of the structure of creativity and its display. In Hebrew it reads: *yehi aur v'yehi aur.* Since Hebrew syntax differs from English, here is a direct translation of the traditional sequencing: Yehi (let there be) Aur (light) V'Yehi (and came to be) Aur (light.)

The numerical values of the words and word combinations of verse 1:3 are listed below. Each will be the subject of an analysis in gematria.

1. The word Yehi (let there be) = 25
2. The word Aur (light) = 207
3. The words Yehi Aur as a statement (let there be light) = 232
4. The word V'Yehi (and came to be) = 31
5. The phrase Yehi Aur V'Yehi Aur (let there be light, and light came to be) = 470

The word *aur* (light) is given twice in this section of the verse. This refers to the two aspects of luminosity: primordial chochmah and manifest chesed. The word *yehi* (*yud-heh-yud*) illustrates this with its two *yuds* on either side of a *heh*. The *heh* represents the Shechinah, which is the central "heart" of the continuum of chochmah and chesed. The presence of the *heh* between these sefirot is graphically illustrated in the Divine Image diagram, with the upper *heh's* horizontal resting between chochmah and chesed.

The word *yehi* simply means "come into being." The first two letters of the word (*yud-heh*) indicate the father and mother union of luminosity and space, which is the Divine Name of chochmah (*YaH*). This is the ultimate wisdom of all appearance. The word "being" used here does not imply that something has come out of nothing "ex nihilo," it simply means that some possibility presents itself. If this is taken beyond the extremes of "something" and "nothing," (the ontological extremes) then there is just open dynamic possibility performing. This is the play of Ain Sof.

The sequence *yud-heh-yud* implies that the *yud* is equal in the beginning of the word as it is in the end, and the *heh* does nothing to change or alter it in any way. This expresses a simultaneity beyond beginning and end. Within continually changing phenomena, nothing essentially changes. There is no thing to change, but still change appears. This is the paradox with which the six days come "into being."

It suggests that phenomenal change is *nullified* to Ain Sof. No matter what appears, nothing but Ain Sof remains.

To nullify a thing brings its sense of separate existence to the zero point. The term used for this in Chassidic and kabbalistic mysticism is *bitul* (nullification). Bitul means that whatever is taken to be "something" can be realized to have no independent existence or autonomous reality whatsoever. To realize that something is bitul nullifies the assertion that it is either real or unreal. The danger in mysticism is that while striving for bitul one can reify nothingness itself. As stated in the introduction, both being and nonbeing can be fixated upon as "solid" conceptions. Bitul is not a rejection of the world. It upholds the intangible paradox of the Divine nature. Bitul seeks to purify cognitive habits that pose a barrier to intangible, substanceless wisdom. Realizing the intense vividness of phenomena as bitul is the main issue dealt with in Genesis 2 and 3, which deal with the Garden of Eden.

The numerical value of *yehi* is 25. This number is produced as the Shechinah (*heh* = 5) reproduces itself in the creative process. The light of creation arises as space expands through "multiplication." Binah and malkut together radiate tension, which multiplies "5 × 5." This arises as light "between the waters." Space and light are co-emergent and simultaneous, as are the *heh* and the *yud*. Thus the light of creation is the result of their "auto-impregnation."

A powerful kabbalistic equation is encoded in the gematria of the phrase *yehi aur* (let there be light), which equals 232. It expresses the wholeness of the Shechinah's spontaneous self-reproduction. This number represents the culmination of all creativity. To understand it properly a little background in kabbalistic theory is necessary.

Each letter of YHVH can be spelled out as a complete word in itself. This process is known as letter expansion. When this is done the numerical value of each expanded letter is calculated into a new gematria, which can then be related to other words. The letters *heh* and *vav* can be spelled out in four different ways. *Heh* also can be spelled *heh-yud, heh-alef,* or *heh-heh. Vav* also can be spelled *vav-yud, vav-alef,* or *vav-vav.* There are four possible expansions of YHVH, each corresponding to a dimension of manifestation, which is the kabbalistic "world" implied by one of its letters. The correspondences can be seen here:

YVD HY VYV HY numerical value: 72 (*yud*-atzilut)

YVD HY VAV HY numerical value: 63 (*heh*-briah)

YVD HA VAV HA numerical value: 45 (*vav*-yetzirah)

YVD HH VV HH numerical value: 52 (*heh*-assiah)

Total = 232

The total numerical value of all four expansions together is 232, which equates with "let there be light." This has profound implications. The four expansions represent the manner in which creativity is fully contextualized. It covers the entire array of the creative process in the fullness of its scope. Equating all light (yehi aur = 232) with the complete scope of its contexts (all four expansions = 232) is an astounding revelation of unity. In the act of manifestation nothing is ever added or subtracted between light and the contexts of its space, which reflects the primordial unity of the seed and womb.

Kabbalistically, there are actually five worlds, the fifth being keter. In the four expansions keter is included within the *yud* as its tip, and thus it has no expansion of its own. Keter is not a distinct world in itself because it is completely bitul to Ain Sof. Therefore, including keter, these are the five aspects and their names:

0. Pristine essence; Ain Sof; tip of *yud*; keter
1. Luminous nature; world of atzilut (72); *yud*; chochmah
2. Axiomatic space; world of briah (63); first *heh*; binah

3. Energy; world of yetzirah (45); *vav*; middle six sefirot
4. Apparitional space; world of assiah (52;) second *heh*; malkut

In the narrative of the first day the word *light* (aur) is mentioned five times. As we know, this is the number of the Shechinah (*heh* = 5). It also corresponds to the five letters of the name *Elohim* (E-L-H-Y-M). This reinforces the notion that light is a wholeness that is expressed as a fivefold variation of phenomena. As stated earlier, the structural implications of the number five articulate the Shechinah's scope in all major areas of phenomena (five worlds, five aspects of mind, five elements, five divisions of the tree, five senses). This fivefold scope is the basis of all creative structures, and will be mentioned again in the account of the second day.

To reiterate, the word for light, *aur,* has a gematria of 207. This equates it with the words *Ain Sof* and *raz* (hidden or secret, which is the disposition of Ain Sof). This illustrates that the radiance of creative motion and its secret primordial basis are essentially equal. The gematria extends radical equanimity into all circumstances that unfold in time. Motion appears to the ordinary mind as the passage of time; however, it is only the mind's habit that makes time. As has been explained, the mind's time habit is fabricated with the construction of temporal reference points that calibrate a conceptual order. Light is that which moves, therefore, and contemplation of the transcendent basis of light nullifies the idea that time and temporal constraints have any independent existence. This is elucidated by Chassidic master Menachem Nahum of Chernobyl:

> Past, present, and future are all unity. That which is to be in the future was already there in the past, before creation. (*Light of the Eyes*)

The *Idra Rabba* section of the *Zohar* gives precious insight into the primordial essentiality of light beyond time in the following quotation:

Everything is in the present, everything is in the past, and everything is in the future. Since there will be no change, and there was no change, there is no change. (*Idra Rabba*)

When the whole statement *yehi aur v'yehi aur* is added up, its total value is 470. This is the gematria of the word *Tanach*, the name for the complete Hebrew Bible. This extraordinary gematria reveals that within the continuum of light, the complete wisdom of the whole Bible is contained. Anyone who takes the Bible as a representation of wisdom would certainly understand this gematria. For those who do not take an absolutist approach to scripture, all we can do is marvel at such intricate interconnections. It certainly is no coincidence.

The gematria of the word *v'yehi* (and came into being) equals 31. This gematria equals the Divine Name *Al* (*alef-lamed*, pronounced "EL"), which corresponds to chesed. This directly equates the unfolding of light "into being" with the expansive and compassionate giving forth of energy.

There is an esoteric adaptation of the letter *heh*, which illustrates the complete scope of Divine chesed. To understand it, Hebrew pronunciation must be clear. Hebrew letters themselves provide consonant sounds. Vowel sounds are indicated by vowel points, which all have sefirotic correspondences. This means that the pronunciation of a word reveals inner sefirotic relationships through the manner in which it is "spoken into existence."

In the *Tikkuney Zohar* a *heh* is described, which illustrates the simultaneity of both supernal and manifest light. This is done by expressing the common bond between them, which is light's nature. The nature of all light is dynamic compassion, or pure chesed. The sefirah of chesed manifests this attribute outright, but the primordial light of the *yud* contains a "secret" supernal aspect of chesed, which is "unmanifest." This is Divine mercy beyond human understanding. This issue has always been one of the greatest mysteries pondered by theologians.

Figure 10

The vowel *segol* corresponds to chesed. The *Tikkuney Zohar*'s *heh* places this vowel in the letter twice, above and below the horizontal (figure 10).

The six days manifest compassion in the aspect "below," but are essentially equal in nature to the primordial source of all compassion "above." This is illustrated by the letter *heh* because the Shechinah is the central heart of both aspects. This has profound relevance to the Divine Image diagram. It suggests the same meaning as the word Yehi, that "before" and "after" creation are essentially equal, and the Shechinah presents that equality in everything that is manifested.

The complete statement *Yehi aur v'yehi aur,* can be arranged vertically in the manner of the Divine Image diagram. The line is divided into two parts, each bearing the words *Yehi aur.* Graphically, the word *yehi* is set vertically, with its two *yuds* above and below the horizontal of its *heh.* The word aur is placed horizontally beneath it (figure 11).

Figure 11

The *yuds* reflect the potential and manifesting aspects of light. Since the manifest aspect actually reveals light, the word *aur* itself is placed horizontally below it.

When laid out as a whole statement this configuration of "yehi aur" is doubled. This illustrates the complete scope of the primordial and manifest aspects of illumination. It must be noted that each "yehi aur" reveals this process as a microcosm. This is also the case with the *heh*s of YHVH, which present the Shechinah's creativity equally, but which are positioned according to context.

Between the two sections of "yehi aur" is a *vav*. In Hebrew the letter *vav* indicates the conjunction and (". . . AND light came to be"). The *vav* binds the two sections in the same manner that the six sefirot of the heaven (*vav* = 6) bind the upper and lower waters.

In this arrangement the horizontals of the *heh*s function exactly as they do in the Divine Image diagram. Thus primordial light extends as manifest light through the *vav,* making a complete YHVH overall. This exactly represents the blueprint of creation laid out in Genesis 1. Thus the configuration represents the equanimity and wholeness between the dimensions "above" and "below." (See figure 12.)

Figure 12

Another graphic element is added to represent the mirrorlike creative activity of Elohim. The upper *heh* has "EL" and "YaM" on either side, forming the name *Elohim* out of its central *heh*. This allows the lower "yehi aur" to graphically indicate the reflection or echo of Elohim's basic creativity. The *vav* represents the reflective motion "between the waters," which is perceptual motion where patterns of cognitive fixation are formed. When the common error of "water-water" is comprehended and internalized, *vav*'s reflective motion is rendered bitul. Then the *vav* reveals the primordial compassion through the light of the first day, which extends the heart of the Shechinah as all phenomena, without ever creating an obstruction or distortion. Thus, through the perfected *vav*, the Shechinah becomes a "perfect mirror" beyond cause and effect.

Rather than transmitting a reflection from "somewhere" to "somewhere else," its mirrorlike wisdom expresses pure simultaneity. It is not merely "mirrorlike," but actually is the mirror itself, as indicated in this often quoted line:

> Their end is imbedded in their beginning and their beginning in their end, like a flame in a burning coal. (*Sefer Yetzirah*)

Fixation to any concept, even the concept of a sefirah, is like "slavery in Egypt." In the same way, the mind can easily become enslaved to a reified concrete definition of god. Grasping at the absolute or any metaphysical precept can turn the sublime intangible Divine essence into an idol, and it thus becomes the grandest form of *idolatry*. Idolatry means placing faith in something that is limited and not ultimately free. Concepts are always limited, even the concept of god and the sefirot. The only way out of this is to be immersed in openness without being held to any concept of reality or unreality. The only way out of this type of idolatry is to go *beyond god*.

The following thirteenth-century quote warns against fixation on the sefirot as separate "powers," and goads the mystic to bind only to Ain Sof:

> Be careful in contemplation not to "cut the shoots," thinking about one sefirah or another. Rather, your thought should be continually unified with Ain Sof, and from there you will spread out and draw

down the branch from your thought to the aspect of YHVH upon which you meditate. The root of your meditation should be continually bound and unified with everything within Ain Sof. Like a flame bound to a burning coal, and grapes on a vine, so all 10 sefirot should be unified in the mind from Ain Sof to Ain Sof. (*Yitzach the Blind*)

The phrase "from Ain Sof to Ain Sof" directly refers to the "before" and "after" aspects of creation. B'reshit is a simple unity above and below. The sefirot can become prisons when the mind is trapped in fixation to their attributes and this wisdom is lost. Each sefirah, like all phenomena, is only an expression of the wonder and majesty of Ain Sof. The only attributes or qualities that pose barriers are those built by the mind's fixations.

Figure 13 illustrates how the sefirot are projections of the *heh*'s horizontal, which is echoed in a hierarchy of ten tzimtzumim. The

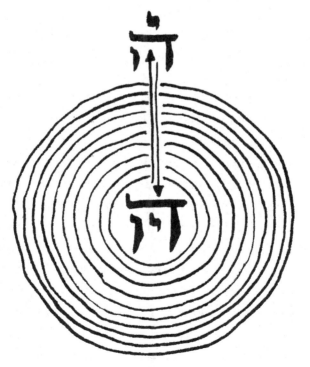

Figure 13

wisdom communicated here is in understanding that the two *heh*s are an inseparable mirrorlike unity, and only the mind's intangible reflections arise between them. This is what is encoded in the word *yehi:* the primordial *yud* is equal "above" and "below" the phenomena that appear to divide it.

DAY 2

(1:6) Elohim said: "Let there be a space in the midst of the waters, and let it divide between waters and waters." (1:7) Elohim made the space, and divided the waters, which were beneath the space from the waters, which were above the space, and it became so. (Gen. 1:6–7)

The second day corresponds to the sefirah of *gevurah*. Its attributes are awe and judgment, and its energetic quality is *contraction*. Contractive motion sets energy within apparitional boundaries. This is the play of tzimtzum at work, which creates intervals within the light of chesed. As the intervals become more and more complex, all the specific patterns that articulate the details of creation become apparent. Intervals that arise within energy are the structural underpinning for what is grasped at as "reality" by sentient beings.

The most fundamental interval is the "separation of the waters." This is the basis of all apparitional illusions, which Rabbi Akiva warned about when he instructed those entering the mystical state not to say "water-water." (See figure 7 on page 53; observe how the names *Elohim* and *Adonai* mark the upper and lower aspects of the waters.) Fixating on a set of intervals allows the illusion of "tangibility" to arise in the mind. Perceptions and ideas are only accepted as real or unreal because a defined impression has been presented and grasped.

Gevurah provides the context that shapes this process. Gevurah's power continually defines phenomena through an endless succession of reflections that appear to divide and fragment. In ordinary cognition this leads directly to the belief in a subject and an object, which spreads out to all phenomena, reducing the play of luminosity and space to the opaque appearance of "substance." This power is referred to as "harsh judgment" in kabbalistic literature. Mitigating this divisive energy at the root of perception is the central issue of human spiritual growth.

Gevurah manifests the paradox of the Shechinah, which is the basic tension between wholeness and multiplicity. This is the tension that shapes perception. Kabbalistic meditation and contemplation purify this tension so that it can express the light of B'reshit rather than serve the attachments and desires of the ego. This is not to say that gevurah is only distorted energy. Like all aspects of creativity, its nature is intangible wisdom. The potency of gevurah reflects cognitive habit. It metes out any tendency. It can serve to articulate the intangible play of visionary appearance or manifest an endless labyrinth of deceptions. Gevurah enforces whatever is required by the mind's condition. It can express the strength of mirrorlike awareness or the weakness of a caged animal.

Gevurah is inherent in the power of choice, which is implicit in human creativity. When it is applied in a clear and decisive manner, the strength of gevurah becomes the energy of discipline. This is employed whenever a specific path is chosen and pursued with conviction. It leads to the wisdom of discernment, which can differentiate true meaningfulness from superficial appeal. These are the paths that lead to the states of *gadlut* (expansive mind) and *katnut* (constricted mind), which are the two "fruits" of the trees in the Garden of Eden.

There is a general unspoken agreement between human beings that is evident in language—that general modes of communication reinforce a common set of assumptions based on the so-called objective structure of reality. This goes unquestioned by almost everyone and perpetuates conventional habits that are continually reinforced by normative social interaction. When human beings consciously or unconsciously agree with the general dualistic habits that obscure the vast equality of space, then gnosis becomes literally impossible. However, the Shechinah always remains stainless and unaffected. The Shechinah is the freedom to either obscure or express its sublime nature.

Rabbi Akiva's edict not to say "water-water" is directly related to mitigating the divisive harshness of gevurah. Not accepting or internally "speaking" falsehood is the first step in passing beyond it. Before the mind can actually change, its errors must be understood. This is incredibly difficult because it contradicts what the physical senses have told the mind since birth. This is elucidated by Rebbe Nachman:

Water-water is the aspect of falsehood, which is the aspect of tears, salty water. When a person drinks salty water not only does he not relieve his thirst, he increases it. He then has to drink other water in order to quench his thirst. This is why falsehood is referred to as water-water. (*Likutey Moharan*)

Cognitive habits are very strong and self-perpetuate by nature. The momentum of habit is formed within the mind's essential dynamism, which is the strongest force in the universe. We get more duality when we drink its "salty water." This only perpetuates suffering, and causes the "tears" that Rebbe Nachman points out. This will unfold later in the Garden of Eden when Eve eats the fruit of the "Tree of Duality" (Good and Evil).

The function of gevurah is the power behind what is called "evil" by religionists. The concept of evil is only that which deceives the mind. This is the imprisoning belief in separation, which perpetuates the habitual momentum of duality. Faith counteracts this tendency by recalling that the prison of dualistic appearances is created from the same luminous space as the infinite bliss of gnosis. In this way faith nullifies the harsh judgments of gevurah.

There is no separate realm of "good" to fight with a realm of "evil." The myth of parallel universes of light and darkness are simply projections of our dualistic tendencies. The seemingly separate intervals that arise within unity are not inherently problematic—only unquestioned belief in the reality of their superficial appearances is. Placing faith in division yields a shattered world. If there is faith in the wholeness of Ain Sof, then it does not matter how many varied impressions come or go; the vast pregnant expanse can always be brought to mind.

The *heh* is one letter, but includes the "separate" graphic form of its left leg, as mentioned previously. Its unity is complete, even though it appears to be divided. Thus the segmented left leg of the *heh* symbolizes gevurah and its capacity to display intervals. This is a profound metaphor for how the Shechinah generates infinite phenomena. In a wider sense, the graphic segmentation of the *heh*'s left leg represents the true nature of tzimtzum, which is intangible wisdom variation.

The separation of the *heh*'s left leg is also analogous to the apparent division of the *heh*s of YHVH. This illusion of division "between the waters" is the basis of the formation of the heavens. Within the space of the heavens the habits of the mind are formed. Thus the broken leg symbolizes the potential for cognitive deception, which is the tendency of water-water, which produces the dualistic "tears" of suffering. This fundamental error allows the concepts of places, things, and events to dominate the mind. Faith in the Shechinah's substanceless wisdom does its repair work here, which allows the *vav* between the *heh*s to be a unifying energy rather than a divisive one. This occurs as gevurah's harsh judgments are tempered.

The Hebrew word for the gap between the waters is *rakia*. This word is usually translated as "firmament," "canopy," or "expanse." All these words denote three-dimensional spatial imagery and imply a sense of "place," which is avoided here by simply using the word "space." Space is contextual by nature, thus it is the master identity of all intervals. This is why verse 1:6 is translated here as: "Let there be a space in the midst of the waters."

In the narrative of the first day the word *aur* was used five times. This expressed that the nature of the all-manifesting light was the Shechinah (*heh* = 5). A similar enumeration happens in the second day, where the word *rakia* is mentioned five times, as is the word *mayim* (waters). This pair of fives suggest the "two hands" (5 fingers each = 10, thus 2 hands = *yud*) that the *Sefer Yetzirah* quote brought up earlier. The light of the first day was a simple and direct expression of the Shechinah. Here, the second day presents the Shechinah in terms of phenomenal contrasts.

The five mentions of the words *mayim* and *rakia* refer to the relationship between the fluid motion of energy (mayim/water) and the contextualizing intervals of space (rakia) that appear to "contain" it. The image that is suggested is that of water being poured into vessels. The vessels are the contexts that arise through tzimtzum. Thus the narrative is depicting what the intervals of the second day appear to do with the simple light of the first day.

In technical kabbalah the relationship between these elements is described in gender terms by the terms *lights* and *vessels*. Generally the term "light" is given to the essential life force of a thing (its "water"), and the term "vessel" refers to the intervals of space, which contextualize it (the aspect of rakia). This is the most common kabbalistic way of communicating how interactive polarity functions, particularly in the Lurianic literature. The narrative is given below with these elements italicized:

(1:6) Elohim said: "Let there be a *space* in the midst of the *waters*, and let it divide between *waters* and *waters*." (1:7) Elohim made the *space* and divided the *waters*, which were beneath the *space* from the *waters*, which were above the *space*, and it became so. (1:8) Elohim called the *space* "heaven." (Gen. 1:6–8)

In a conventional sense, light is *what knows* and its contextualizing vessel defines *what is known*. Under ordinary circumstances, tzimtzum imposes boundaries that render phenomena dull, opaque, and impenetrable. What is frustrating is that this persists while the struggle for a more expansive view is being cultivated. Perception becomes heavy and coarse, and a dim lusterless facade of ordinary fixation takes over everything. This manifests through the polar interaction of "lights and vessels," which allows the vast expanse of luminous space to assume the role of a *barrier* in the mind, exactly the opposite of what it truly is. This is referred to by the Chabad Rebbe:

> The concept of tzimtzum and concealment is the aspect of "vessels," while the life force itself is the aspect of "light." Just as a vessel conceals something inside it, the tzimtzum covers and conceals the light that is transmitted. These vessels are the letters of the Hebrew alphabet. (*Tanya, Shaar HaYichud VeHaEmunah*)

The miraculous thing is that human beings can still intuit the brilliance of vast luminosity to some degree. It manages to sparkle through during moments of intense joy and vivid relaxation. Unfortunately these rare glimpses disappear as soon as habitual fixation reasserts itself, which usually occurs almost immediately.

Cultivating compassion, which is the expansive light of chesed, can mitigate gevurah's constricting force. This nullifies the conflict between "light and vessel" and restores unity. Both light and vessel lose the illusion of being independent identities, and they become bitul to their actual nature. In kabbalistic literature the restraining influence is said to be broken through, and the "sparks" of indwelling luminosity contained in the "shells" of the tzimtzum constraints are liberated into freedom.

When a vessel succeeds in obscuring light it is referred to as a *klipah* or "hard shell." These barriers arise within physical, emotional, intellectual, or spiritual contexts. *Klipot* are synonymous with the forces of "evil," and thus division. They are always products of perceptual habit. They arise from an imbalance of gevurah when phenomenal space is engaged with a stance of "existential combat." Layers upon layers of klipot define ordinary cognition. Spiritual purification is the stripping away of these concealments. Breaking the habit of holding phenomena to be impenetrable is enormously difficult. Forcing the issue accomplishes nothing. Klipot only become free as the mind relaxes into the spacious love of the Shechinah, in a return to the expansive chesed, which is innate to space. More than any intellectual gymnastics, what liberates the sparks from the klipot is simple devotion to wholeness beyond conventional extremes.

The end of the *Tanya* quote given above refers to the Hebrew letters as "Holy vessels." A Holy vessel is a necessary aspect of creativity that expresses the paradox of the Shechinah. Letters differentiate and adapt creative differences to display the variation of speech. Speech is the ultimate kabbalistic metaphor for the creative process. Thus the letters that constitute speech represent how the basic tension between unity and diversity is negotiated. This requires the specificity of intervals, which are embodied by the letters. Through their variation the infinite phenomena of the four worlds arises.

It is the wholeness of Ain Sof that "speaks," of course. As Shechinah (the display of phenomena), Ain Sof is the speaker and the speech. This unity flows directly through the human mind. Through devotion, Divine speech and human prayer can converge and become bitul to each other. When this happens the indwelling sparks of phenomena are liberated, and a tremendous reversal of klipot can be achieved. This is the underlying goal in Chassidic prayer, which is articulated in the following quote from Chassidic master R. Zechariah of Yereslav:

> When you pray you should have in mind to arouse all the letters
> with which heaven and earth were created. If you do this all the
> worlds will join in your prayer, arousing the letters, which are the

life-force of all creation. Then all things in both heaven and earth will be included in your prayer. (*Darkey Tzedek*)

When kabbalists speak of this process it applies to every possible aspect of cognizance in which spiritual work is accomplished, not merely verbal prayer in the physical sense. The unfettered expression of the fire of the Shechinah makes all vessels bitul to their light, and all words bitul to the essential silence in which they are spoken. The light of Ain Sof both fills and surrounds all constructs, and is inherent in all of space. The quotation above suggests that the Shechinah should simply be realized as the ground of whatever happens. This should be remembered when faced with situations that seem to block or repel the mind. Love can radiate so strongly that its blazing can nullify these barriers and actualize radiance that is beyond understanding. This process is completely nonintellectual and consists of pure intensity. Whether through the methods of prayer (right), contemplation (left), or pure meditative stability (center), this intensity can be cultivated. Faith that this is so is based on believing the words of the tzaddikim, such as in this quote by Rebbe Nachman:

The light of the heart's flaming reaches all the way to Ain Sof. (*Likutey Moharan*)

Gevurah enforces creative precepts, whatever they may be, for better or for worse. It sets the fire of binah into motion. This fire can take the form of sublime love or utter devastation. The Shechinah's unity is like the nurturing love of a mother. It transcends all boundaries. It is the sense within us that we are surrounded by love. This can be totally overwhelming. When the Shechinah's omnipresence is met with devotion they both become nullified by each other. In this way devotion can actually liberate the mind's motion held by the klipah-barriers that define any constricted state. This is life as prayer, which is a way of living and not just an obtuse metaphor.

Each imprisoned spark is an aspect of wholeness that has no independent existence. It is just an opportunity for return to primordial unity. If the force of gevurah is approached with this view, then its might can be a guide to the sweetening of all phenomena. This means that whatever appears structurally in the world can be held as the play of the chesed of the Shechinah. This elevates gevurah to binah, which is the boundless source of all chesed and the light of the first day. This is expressed by Rebbe Nachman:

> The method for chasing away the external forces (klipot) is to draw the gevurot from the root of binah into the knees. (*Likutey Moharan*)

The "knees" represent the interactive functions of mental analysis and decisive activity, which "carry" our attention. They correspond to the sefirot of *hod* and *netzach*. These components lead the mind to choices that can change its point of view, and thus lead to new directions. Purifying apparitional space begins with intention carried by the "knees." What the great tzaddikim achieved began with the simple desire to grow. They are not essentially different from us. They have just done the work. The message of the Baal Shem Tov can be summarized by the words of his great grandson (Rebbe Nachman): "All people can be tzaddikim just like me." However, this takes many years of dedicated, painful spiritual practice, which few are willing to tolerate.

DAY 3

The third day presents the sefirah of *tiferet,* whose attributes are beauty and harmonious balance. Tiferet expresses the cohesiveness of energy, as a continuous spectrum integrating the expansive tendencies of chesed and the contractive tendencies of gevurah. Tiferet reflects the whole of creative motion, and is the sefirah that symbolizes the complete scope of the "heavens." The *Zohar* states:

Light on the right side and darkness on the left. What did the Holy One do? He combined them and created the heavens from them. What are the heavens? Fire and water. He combined them and made peace between them. When they were brought together they were stretched out like a curtain, He stretched them out and made the letter vav. (*Zohar*)

The word for the "heavens" is *shemayim,* spelled *shin-mem-yud-mem.* The word can be deconstructed to illustrate a balance between fire and water, the primary elements of manifestation. The letter *shin* represents the self-consuming fire of the Shechinah, and the letters *mem-yud-mem* spell out the letter name of *mem,* which symbolizes water. Thus the word can be read as "fire-water," expressing the unity of the water of the right side and the fire of the left. The *Zohar* quotation then states that fire and water are unified by harmony or "peace," which is "stretched out like a curtain." This suggests that the continuum of creative energy is all-pervasive and without boundaries, equal to all of space.

Tiferet is the focal point of the six middle sefirot and is considered their "heart," therefore, it corresponds to the *vav* of YHVH. In the Divine Image diagram tiferet is the only sefirah that actually touches the *vav.* This diagrammatically reinforces its role as mediator of the balance of the six sefirot. This is also symbolized by the numerical value of *vav* (*vav* = 6), which equates with tiferet (the sixth sefirah).

On the tree, tiferet marks the midpoint between keter and malkut. Energetic motion is often described as bi-directional oscillation between these vectors: it "descends" from above to below and "ascends" from below to above. This characterizes energetic motion from the perspective of human thought. It manifests as birth and dissolves as death, in a cyclical manner. All mental constructs go through this cycle. The phenomena of the mind appear and then dissolve. This is the apparitional play of Ain Sof.

The "descent" into manifestation draws cognizance into the field of perception. This is referred to in Hermetic texts as the "involutionary" direction of energy. It displays and presents phenomena. The "ascent" is its "evolutionary" counterpart. This is the capacity for the mind to grow beyond its limitations toward its primordial nature. These terms obviously reflect a dualistic point of view, but successfully describe how motion is conventionally perceived. Kabbalistic texts refer to this activity as running and returning, after a phrase in Ezekiel chapter 1, which describes the *merkavah,* or chariot of mystical ascent. It refers to the oscillating motion of the mind, which continually presents and dissolves phenomena. Mastering this cyclical motion is the basis of much of meditation.

Under most circumstances the mind is beset with layers and layers of constrictions and limitations. When a barrier is broken through, the mind is allowed to "run" into more expansive territory until it hits another barrier. Then it settles into the territory that has been uncovered and it "returns" to stabilize there, until it runs again. With arduous effort the mind can run further and further as it grows. The "returning" deepens exponentially with the running. Through this interchange, perception can be pushed through ever more subtle territory, and can become conditioned to transcend its habituated constraints. Ultimately, running and returning unfold into the silent expanse of space. This is the basis of the mind's "speech," as directly referred to in the following quote:

> Ten Sefirot of nothingness: Bridle your mouth from speaking and your heart from thinking. If your heart runs, return to the place, as written: "The Chayot running and returning." Regarding this a covenant was made. (*Sefer Yetzirah*)

The running and returning takes place "between the waters," in what the *Zohar* calls "six steps." This maps out the complete range between the upper and lower aspects of the Shechinah, where the attributes of energy are formed. It states:

It is written: "Six steps to the throne." Six to the upper throne and six to the lower throne. (*Zohar Hadash*)

The number six articulates the spatialization of movement, which is how conventional cognition orients itself. Six directions (up, down, front, back, right, left) articulate how motion becomes extended from a central point. Each direction is a vector through which the oscillating motion of running and returning becomes possible. Thus sixfold motion creates six spatial contexts, which illustrate the interdependence of motion and space. Motion cannot move without space contextualizing it. Conventionally, this describes "where" motion goes. On a deeper level, it reveals that the Shechinah is the omnipresent basis of all motion. Equating basic space with motion is implied in the name binah (BeN YaH = the sixfold son of Yah).

The Shechinah is the essential presence that radiates as sixfold motion. It is also the surrounding space into which the six directions flow. This is the unity of the ocean water (YaM), which both flows and accepts the flowing. Thus the Shechinah is the "all-inclusive heart" of phenomena. As mentioned earlier, tiferet is also referred to as the "heart" of the heavens. This is no contradiction. The Shechinah pours creative motion out without ever leaving its own vastness. The Shechinah is the "heart presence" of tiferet. The Shechinah manifests the omnipresence of keter, which appears everywhere but cannot be contained anywhere, as the rabbis of the Talmud informed the Athenian wise men. The *Zohar* states:

(From B'reshit) the six great supernal mysteries are engraved from which all derives. From them six fountains and streams are made so that they might be poured into a great sea. This is the meaning of BaRA ShYT (six are created). (*Zohar*)

The fact that the word *B'reshit* can be read as "six are created" is an important clue to what perceptual motion really is. Linking B'reshit with "six fountains" reveals that directionality only extends the nature of the mind's basic dynamism. This is the sole "Fountain of Wisdom" that allows gnosis to arise within the cognitive act. Once realized, it cannot be disrupted by any appearance or directional coordinate.

No matter how it becomes contextualized, energy always "runs and returns." Consider the waveform manner in which energy is expressed. Frequencies of energy are formed by an oscillation between polar tendencies. Energy itself is the continuum of tiferet, but its intervals arise through the serpentine interplay of chesed (positive) and gevurah (negative). The tension set between these poles determines how its attributes are "tuned," no matter what the context (i.e., color, sound, thought, emotion, etc.). These oscillations constitute the undulating body of the serpent, which is the basic tension inherent in energetic expression. Remember this when the serpent appears in Eden in the third chapter of Genesis.

The relationship between energy and space is referred to in terms of a marriage. The six sefirot are referred to as *Zer Anpin*, which is the aspect of the "husband." The bride is malkut, referred to as his *Nukva*. The relationship between the partners is characterized by degrees of maturity. In a state of complete maturity the pair are described as inseparably bound in the sexual reproductive union called *zivug*. A mature zivug perfectly reflects the primordial union of chochmah and binah (the father and mother union of luminosity and basic space). Either this supernal unity is realized within the play of Zer Anpin and Nukva or it is not. In a state of immaturity the marriage partners only relate to each other in degrees. Later kabbalistic texts calibrate gnosis through the degree of intimacy Zer Anpin and Nukva display, whether they are "face-to-face," "back-to-back," or whether they "kiss." Ultimately, this imagery describes how deeply consciousness has realized (or not realized) the mystical state of bitul.

The relationship between Zer Anpin and Nukva is completely interdependent. This nullifies the assumption that either partner has any independent existence. There can be no wife without a husband, and can be no husband without a wife. The marriage arises as the partners come together to define each other. Recognizing the interdependence of the zivug is the same as bitul. In their transcendent union the marital partners merge together beyond existence or non-existence. Realizing this is the nature of our own mind and its phenomena is the goal of spiritual maturation. It is why the sexual imagery of the "Song of Songs" is considered the ultimate mystical statement. Zivug renders both perceiver and its perceptions bitul, and all concrete designations such as inner and outer, self and world, simply dissolve. As such, neither "part" nor "whole" can be taken to have any independent existence whatsoever.

> (1:9) Elohim said: "Let the waters beneath the heaven be gathered into one place, and let dryness be seen," and it became so. (1:10) Elohim called the dryness "earth" and the gathering of waters he called "seas," and Elohim saw that it was good. (Gen. 1:9–10)

In the narrative of the third day the co-emergent dance of energy and space is characterized by the symbols of *dryness* and *water*. Together they articulate the illusory continuum of stability and change. "Dry" refers to fixed appearances, which seem to remain constant (although nothing ever does). This is indicated when "dry earth is seen," indicating that form is perceived (seen) as continuous and discrete. This term is often used in alchemical texts to portray the state of solidity of a substance. "Wetness" represents the appearance of transformation. What is "wet" is fluid in disposition, thus wetness is the aspect of phenomenal change in which motion is perceived. In this context the "sea" refers to the totality of unfixed volatility, which is the nature of all energy. This term is common in alchemy as well, dating back to the earliest known alchemical tracts. In contrast to the "sea," the "dry earth" represents solid matter. Between them all possible creative variables arise.

The earth brought forth grass, herbs yielding seed of its kind, and trees bearing fruit which has in it seeds of its kind. (Gen. 1:12)

The complete scope of energy is then referred to with a calibrated series of organic symbols that articulate its complexity. Three levels are suggested, which are symbolized by types of vegetation: grass, herbs with seed, trees bearing fruit containing seed. Each stage refers to a process in which energy is expended. Grass symbolizes the simplest function of energy: to grow and be consumed by the beasts of the field. Herbs that bear seed have the added dimension of visibly self-generated reproduction: seeds that perpetuate the species. Because of this they represent cyclical patterns of energy. The trees are the most complex in their implication. The tree's fruit seeds perpetuate cyclical growth in the manner of herbs, but the fruit also nourishes human creativity and provides energy that ultimately becomes the human mind. Therefore the tree represents the pinnacle of vegetative growth.

The three energetic stages refer to degrees of temporal subtlety in perception. Each stage extends the previous one. Grass grows to be consumed, processed, and its waste expelled. It represents the superficial "food of the moment," which is completely transitory. The animals that eat grass are bound only to immediate temporal circumstances that express simplistic linear motion. The seeded herbs refer to self-perpetuating cycles such as birth and death, the seasons, and the ebb and flow of external appearances. With the herb, time becomes a circle rather than a line. The minds of most human beings are locked within these cycles and few see beyond them. It is the self-perpetuating fruit of the tree that extends cyclical energy into spiritual growth. This allows human life to approach its essential Divinity. Its fruit is the food of human evolution. This significant aspect allows the symbol of the fruit tree to take on an extremely important role in the narrative of the Garden of Eden in chapter three.

✴

The account of the third day begins with the edict: "Let the waters be gathered beneath the heavens into one place." The concept of "one place" designates the Shechinah as the sole space that contextualizes and equalizes all things. Most kabbalists take the one place to refer to malkut, but it refers to the Shechinah in a wider sense. The Shechinah gathers motion into appearance; however, motion itself is not other than Shechinah. All designations (such as "where" a place is or "what" kind of motion it displays) ultimately refer back to the interdependent zivug of tiferet and malkut. This is the metaphorical "gathering" of the supernal water that makes up the lower marriage.

The gathering collects "beneath the heavens." This is a reference to malkut, which is graphically placed "beneath" the six aspects of motion. In a diagrammatic sense this is where appearances appear. However, malkut's display is only a "gathering" of the basic ubiquitous expanse of Ain Sof, the true essence of the Shechinah. Energy does not congeal into "something" and arise "somewhere." The heart of kabbalistic mysticism nullifies these concepts. The simultaneity of context and energy simply arises to ornament the glory of its nature. This is the true essence of the zivug.

In the Divine Image diagram, malkut is graphically suspended under the horizontal of the lower *heh,* flanked by its right and left legs. The sefirah does not touch any part of the letter. This graphic placement symbolizes how forms appear "isolated" in conventional perception. The two legs of the lower *heh* illustrate the expansive and contractive tendencies that shape the reflections that perception clings to. As beings hold malkut's reflections to be separate, the lower waters are taken to be a world of real things that exist "under heaven." When this occurs in the mind, phenomena assumes the role of tangible substance in the minds of beings.

The triad of chesed, gevurah, and tiferet is known by the acronym *ChaGaT.* The triad of ChaGaT is a set of pure energetic tendencies:

expansive, contractive, and harmonious. The expansion of chesed knows no contraction, and the contraction of gevurah is only involved in constrictive activity. Tiferet's harmony is not a composite in the sense that two separate things are combined in it. Tiferet is the simultaneity of the expansive and contractive possibilities. In the space of manifestation these possibilities do not obstruct or conflict with one another. They represent open adaptation and endless variation.

This continuum of ChaGaT's phenomenal harmony is communicated by the central kabbalistic symbol of the rainbow (*Qeshet*). The rainbow is described in the *Zohar* as a combination of three colors: the white of chesed, the red of gevurah, and the yellow of tiferet (often mistranslated as green). These three colors merge in the next triad of netzach, hod, and yesod (NeHiY). There they produce the mixed colors of light and dark salmon pink (hod and netzach) and a purple made of all the colors together (yesod), which incorporates the blue of space (malkut). These are the color attributions that the early kabbalists and the *Zohar* use, although later kabbalists use a different system based on primary and secondary colors.

The rainbow represents lucent cognitive purity as phenomenal display. It offers human beings the possibility of an alternative to the dense and opaque appearance of ordinary consciousness. When cognizant lucency has become dim and claustrophobic, the rainbow reminds us of the most sublime aspects of visionary perception.

In Genesis chapter 9 Noah sealed a bond with god, and was shown the rainbow as its sign. The following passage is of monumental kabbalistic importance as a metaphor for gnosis and the expression of the zivug of tiferet and malkut:

> Elohim said: "This is the sign of the covenant (brit) that I pledge between myself and you, and between every living creature that is with you for the generations of all time. I have set my rainbow in the clouds, and it shall be a sign of the covenant between myself and the

earth. At a time when I bring clouds over the earth the rainbow will be seen in the clouds. I shall remember my covenant that is between myself and you and between every living soul in all flesh, that never again will flood waters destroy all flesh. The rainbow shall be seen in the clouds and I will see her and remember the everlasting covenant." (Gen. 9:12–16)

The rainbow is one of the most profound kabbalistic symbols for visionary consciousness. It expresses the manner in which cognition arises as human perception realizes its intrinsic bond with Divinity. The rainbow reminds us that so-called ordinary reality can be dwarfed by possibilities that are brighter and subtler than any of our fixations. It saturates the expanse of the sky with luminous color, directly implying the zivug of luminosity and space. This display is immaterial and insubstantial, but it paradoxically appears in a pristine vivid form. Most importantly, the rainbow manifests *beauty*. "Beauty" is the literal translation of the word tiferet. These attributes invite the mind to contemplate the inner magic of creative phenomena, which call mediocrity into question and can obliterate any toleration of the cognitive status quo.

The rainbow has a very complex kabbalistic attribution. There are three main ways to attribute it to the sefirot. The first is that the rainbow corresponds to malkut. It symbolizes a pure view of the "space of all things known." This implies that all appearance, which we take to be tangible and divided, can be intangible, substanceless, and bright. The second attribution equates the rainbow with tiferet. This is easy to understand, because tiferet manifests cooperative resonant beauty, and gathers all motion into a harmony like the rainbow's colors. The third correspondence is the key between these two. It equates the rainbow with yesod. Yesod is the point of integration between the six sefirot and malkut. This is where light and space manifest their union, thus yesod is associated with the consummation (zivug) of the Divine marriage.

Yesod corresponds to the genitals and is the site of the *brit* (circumcision). The word "brit" also means "covenant." As the "seal of the covenant" mentioned in Noah, the rainbow symbolizes the bond between the mind's perceptual motion and the phenomena it perceives. This is analogous to the bond between human beings and god. The mystical connotation is that the union of perceiver and perceived is insubstantial, luminous, spacious, and beautiful. Thus the rainbow combines the beauty of the visionary state with bitul, the insubstantial wisdom nature of all phenomena.

The rainbow, therefore, marks the interdependent bond between tiferet and malkut *through* yesod. This integration represents how manifestation actually works. It is the "one place" where ChaGaT becomes sensually apprehended as the ultimate expression of the Shechinah. Rebbe Nachman articulates this in one of his greatest teachings:

> Judgment is mitigated through song, as written in the Holy Zohar: "The rainbow is the Shechinah." The three colors of the rainbow are the patriarchs, who are the garments of the Shechinah. (*Likutey Moharan*)

The rainbow is the ultimate expression of the Shechinah because it reveals the perfect integration of motion and space. As an earlier *Zohar* quote mentioned, creative motion and space are a unity like "streams flowing into the ocean." In this sense the rainbow's beauty leads directly into the contemplation of the intangible wisdom of Ain Sof in the purest sense.

The rainbow is an appearance that has no obscurity or opacity. It is only a garment for the apprehension of purity, wonder, and joy. It is a model of what perception can be when the mind's nature breaks free of its klipot. When the spark of gnosis is raised from concealment the rainbow is always revealed. This marks the visionary transformation of the dullness and opacity of ordinary circumstance. The rainbow offers no conceptual equivalence or external agenda. Its simple spacious brilliance *is* its meaning. Its intangible beauty will arise later to describe the universe as the Garden of Eden, which is a display of the mystical rainbow in the deepest sense.

As Rebbe Nachman points out, the kabbalistic rainbow consists of three colors that correspond to the three biblical patriarchs. The patriarchs personify the sefirot of ChaGaT within the biblical narrative. Abraham corresponds to chesed, Isaac to gevurah, and Jacob to tiferet. In the Bible the lives of the patriarchs were completely dedicated to serving the visionary beauty of the Shechinah, and stand as examples to all humanity of how to live in vivid purity while living in complete surrender (bitul) to the Divine.

The use of the word "song" in Rebbe Nachman's quote is significant. Song is a harmonization of sound in the same manner that the rainbow harmonizes color. However, sound implies the specific context of prayer. In Jewish liturgy the recitation of the Torah is sung to melodies that correspond to kabbalistic notations. This aspect of "wisdom song" allows the notes (which are the actual words of the text) to become radiant and soar through space. In a visionary sense, this turns the auditory dimension of Torah into a realm of sonorous vastness, like "streams pouring into the sea."

Rebbe Nachman states there can be a "mitigation of judgment by song." This refers to the harshness of gevurah becoming "sweetened" through recognition of harmonious wisdom. Like the rainbow, "song" describes the beautiful inner nature of phenomena. The position of true faith is that whatever the mind apprehends is the radiant display of Ain Sof. Faith and devotion alchemically transform perception into prayer, thus phenomena become both "song" and "rainbow."

Formal prayer allows letters to be combined to express spiritual longing. Tradition holds that all of heaven and earth are metaphorically comprised of such letters. Therefore the melody of mystical prayer can be expressed as anything, and any cognitive act can become a Holy song that mirrors the subtle brilliance of the visionary state. The mitigation of gevurah's harshness arises through faith in the "basic wondrousness" of life. This is completely dependent upon intention. A great tzaddik once said: "The intention to have faith itself causes faith."

Later Rebbe Nachman goes on to attribute the triad ChaGaT to the three basic elements of manifestation: water (right), fire (left), and air (center). It states:

> The sounds of song are the three colors of the rainbow, for the voice consists of fire, water, and wind. These are the three patriarchs, the patriarchs being the three radiant colors in whom "I will see her and remember the everlasting covenant." (*Likutey Moharan*)

The appearance of the physical rainbow involves the light of the sun, moisture in the atmosphere, and the air in which they interact. These elements also typify the voice that sings out devotion to Ain Sof: the heat of the heart, moisture of the breath, and the air of the breath. These aspects of the rainbow allow us to understand how microcosm (human song) and macrocosm (the harmony of the elements) can resonate together to realize a common expression.

Rebbe Nachman is pointing out how the klipah-barriers that obscure yesod dissolve through the joy of pure phenomena. This is what the covenant actually does. When the "cosmic genitalia" is cleared of all obstructing conceptual and perceptual obscurations the clarity and depth of phenomena shine unreservedly. This equates with peeling the foreskin from the penis of a Jewish boy. In Genesis 9 this corresponds to the rainbow appearing through the "clouds," which are the obscuring klipot. The image of the rainbow shining through this barrier conveys the power of wisdom to "outshine" its obscurations. This is the promise that the tzaddik brings, which is sealed in the bond between our actual condition and the potential of what we can be if we allow ourselves to grow beyond dualizing extremes.

The rainbow's appearance signifies the completion of the "flood." The flood is a literary symbol for the purification of the earth, which is Shechinah. The water of the flood is mind, and the earth is its apparitional display. Noah corresponds with yesod, where they connect—he personifies the integration of the mind's flowing motion with the display of its phenomena, which is the zivug of the Divine marriage. At yesod the covenant can be sealed and the visionary rainbow realized. Thus Noah represents the archetypal tzaddik, and is considered to be the first incarnation of Moses.

The flood of mind is only "destructive" in relation to the klipot of conventional perception. Their purification facilitates the apprehension of beauty and joy (i.e., the rainbow). This is the universal message of all tzaddikim, expressed by the Baal Shem Tov:

> One should serve God with both awe and joy, as they are "two friends who never part." (*Tzava'as HaRivash*)

This profound quotation is a play on a phrase from the *Zohar*: "two friends who never part," which refers to chochmah and binah. Its implication is that supernal wisdom clothes itself in the pure emotional attributes of ChaGaT: awe is the aspect of gevurah and joy is the aspect of chesed. These feelings both accompany the apprehension of great beauty, which is tiferet. The suggestion is that visionary brilliance perfectly harmonizes the two sides, and in that union the innate wisdom of the upper waters is expressed as the fabric of perception. This is how supernal wisdom is clothed within the vivid perceptual display of the rainbow. It is an astoundingly simple synopsis of a process that is indescribably complex.

The following illustration, by seventeenth-century Hermetic Qabbalist Robert Fludd (figure 14) depicting the *vav* as the extension of the *yud*, expresses the continuity between perceptual motion and primordial wisdom. The *vav* is the balance between two pans of a scale, each representing one of the *heh*s of YHVH. The *vav* either facilitates balance or imbalance between them. In the diagram the imbalance of conventional cognition is apparent, as the lower *heh* (the darker one) weighs heavy and tips the scale.

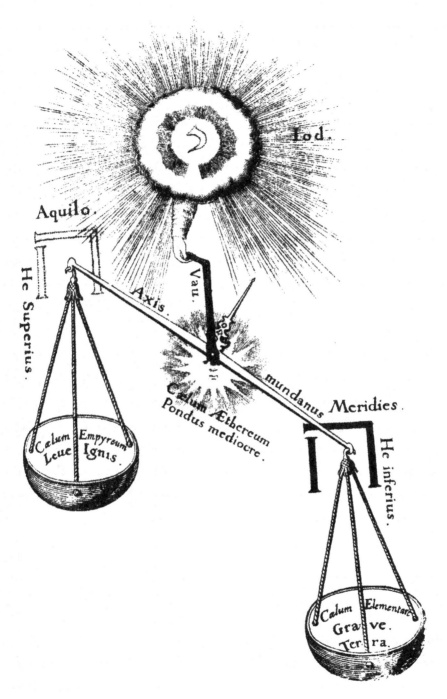

Figure 14

DAYS 4 AND 5

Days four and five correspond to the sefirot of netzach and hod. They will be described together because they express a unique mutual dependence, and appear as a unit in much of kabbalistic literature. Often they are included with yesod, referred to as triad *NeHiY* (netzach/hod/yesod).

Netzach and hod are the aspects of expansive and contractive energies that are applied within the ever-changing circumstances of phenomena. Within the continuum of ordinary perception, each moment and mental object is set in relation to all others. Netzach and hod are the aspects of action and analysis that engage these elements. They are mechanisms at the front line of the search for meaning and experience, which penetrate situations and excavate conclusions.

Netzach and hod apply creativity and choice in accordance with intention. As a result of this they are at the crossroads of two vectorial directions. They can be applied to sustain the ordinary fixation on relativity or they can be employed to break through its barriers to become bitul to its essential nature. Both directions express intention, which is the overall disposition that guides a process. Netzach and hod are only tools that facilitate that process. When incorporated in the service of Divine realization, netzach and hod are called "the gates of prophecy." In the ordinary sense they represent the desire to search out information and experience and to analyze whatever has been sought.

Respectively, netzach applies the expansive action of the right side to penetrate phenomena and hod applies the contractive action of the left side to reduce it to a conclusion or impression. Thus netzach and hod are conduits for ChaAaT, and bring their interactivity into a "mixed" circumstance. Netzach expands, but only in a context that has been defined by a set of limits. Hod contracts, but only in the wake of a specific aspect of expansive energy that has been contextualized. The kabbalist Aryeh Kaplan likens this relationship to a traffic light. Green signifies "go," but it is not an open command to go without regulation; it is conditional. One can only go within the context of a forthcoming anticipated stopping point (the light will turn red eventually). The same is true for its opposite. Go and stop are therefore tempered with each other in a relationship where each can only be expressed in the other's presence. In this way the echo of chesed and gevurah conforms to the interdependency inherent in apparitional circumstance.

Netzach and hod are referred to as the "legs" of the Divine Image because they carry creative motion on to a path. This designation also relates them to the legs of the *heh*. The legs of the *heh* shape the view that manifests through its horizontal "window." The shaping of its phenomena involves expansive and contractive activity that endlessly mixes its reflections. Beings perceive these mixed reflections in accordance with their habits. If there are no klipot making the reflections impermeable, then there are no attachments to habituate. In the absence of constrictive habits, whatever appears through the *heh*'s window is recognized as *equal in nature* to the open expanse above its horizontal. The fact that beings fixate on "something" is an indication that this openness is cluttered with attachments to the constant interchange of expanding and contracting reflections that echo endlessly in space. The question of netzach and hod's status in shaping these reflections is just a question of habituation. Like all good tools, their efficacy depends on how they are used.

In the Divine Image diagram netzach and hod correspond with the termination points of the legs of the upper *heh*. It may seem that they should be attached to the lower *heh* instead because they are directly involved with the contextualization of malkut. However, this graphic device suggests something profound.

The formative motion of the heavens directly extends the pure undivided space of binah (binah = Ben Yah). Therefore all the right and left sefirot of the heavens are bound to the upper *heh*, even though their reflections are grasped at within a seemingly separate lower *heh*. But the endless hall of mirrors that is attributed to malkut is not separate from binah. Malkut, and the heavenly energies that form it, both project the

Shechinah equally. The creative potency of the supernal water echoes throughout space, and the sum of its echoes are apprehended as malkut. Faith can serve to remind and reinforce the fact that basic space and its contexts are a continuous unity. Taking absolute and relative positions to be separate completely undermines the radical equanimity that renders all epistemological and ontological distinctions bitul.

Fleeting mental impressions, which seem real and lasting, are continually grasped at by the senses. Ultimately, they are all as impermanent and insubstantial as the image of the moon reflected on the surface of a pond. A common mistake that spiritual aspirants make is to believe that these impressions are like a "skin" covering over the deeper aspects of the creative process. This is not so. All the mind's phenomena express the Divine nature of Ain Sof, even when it becomes distorted and misapprehended. Certainly we should not trust whatever the mind spits out, but we can have faith that its nature is only the nuptial play of luminosity and spaciousness. It is always an invitation into radiant vastness and is always displayed with the colors of the rainbow.

Variation arises as malkut reflects infinite facets of cognitive habit that arise between the waters. These are intangible ripples, but easily become thick klipot if we reify and grasp at them. The mechanism that actually makes contact and engages every nuance of phenomena is the triad of NeHiY. This is where the most insidious habits take root. If they are purified, the triad of NeHiY can seek and recognize the water of its own nature, rendering binah, malkut, and the heavens all bitul to Ain Sof. If there are no attachments to habituate, then NeHiY reveals the purity of the rainbow's song, and it unfolds "clothed" within the triad ChaGaT. This unifies both triads, creating the state of Ruach Ha-Kodesh (Holy ruach), which is the complete integration of awareness into the scope of the six sefirot. In Chassidic terminology, this is called *mochin d'gadlut* (expanded consciousness).

An earlier *Zohar* quote mentioned that space conforms to energetic motion, creating "six chambers" in the heavens. In the mystical ascent the mind does not "pass through" malkut to get there. The chambers are openings into the vastness of the Shechinah, which the NeHiY triad becomes absorbed within. Each degree of subtlety allows NeHiY to carry awareness deeper into the alchemical marriage of light and space. In this manner perceptual motion literally "walks" into its own structure.

> Elohim said: "Let there be lights in the space of the heaven to divide between the day and the night, and they will serve for omens for seasons for days and for years." (Gen. 1:14)

The fourth day corresponds to netzach. It begins: "Let there be lights in the space (rakia) of the heaven." Its "lights" mark the extension of chesed into netzach. The context of the "rakia of the heaven" implies a "rakia within a rakia." This is the triad of NeHiY, which is set within the greater scope of the sixfold heavens. There tzimtzum is applied to the endless multiplicity of circumstance, implied by the plural term "lights." This defines the variation of netzach's force. Energetic variation erupts throughout the open field of space to include both external events like the shining of stars as well as internal events like emotional impressions. Every energetic discharge, from the production of a single cell to the shining of infinite suns, is included in the continuum of the fourth day.

The lights of the fourth day set their variation within the momentum and continuity of chesed, which is the general energy of manifestation. This is indicated in the Divine Image diagram—the right leg of the upper *heh* that connects netzach directly with chesed and the *heh*'s horizontal. This illustrates that netzach's energetic momentum is the extension of the Ruach Elohim. This is visible in ordinary perception, where continuity perpetuates and drives habit. Once a cognitive pattern is established, it carries its dynamic forward and it grows in self-reinforcing potency until some interference causes it to stop. The momentum of habit is no more evident than in the case of our perception of time. We have implicit faith in the unfolding of our temporal impressions simply because our time habit has accumulated such enormous momentum. Most human beings never question this. Temporality is the very foundation of ordinary thinking.

The line "[the lights] will serve for omens for seasons for days and for years" suggests that subtle meanings can be dissevered within temporal motion. This is the basis of astrology. Astrological omens are marked through relationships between heavenly bodies, revealing connections between their cycles and physical events. The omens can open deeper connections between energy and perception on an inner level. They point out patterns within cognition that indicate what we have been and what we will be in the passage of time.

> Elohim made the two great lights, the large to rule the day and the small to rule the night, and the stars. Elohim set them in the space of the heaven to illuminate the earth. (Gen. 1:16–17)

The two great lights refer to the sun and the moon. These symbols are the root of all relationships. This is mentioned on the fourth day because light's variation operates through interdependent contrasts. The basis of all contrast is the union of chochmah and binah, expressed through a continuous stream of polar activity.

The word netzach translates as "victory." Its function is to perpetuate momentum. Netzach allows energy to break through barriers, thus producing "victory" over constraints. In contrast, chesed has no such barriers. This is the difference between the light of the first day and the application of that light within the relative relationships of the fourth day. As right side sefirot, what distinguishes netzach from chesed is the influence of gevurah from the left. Netzach's push toward "victory" can only emerge in relation to a counterforce that tries to restrain it. The job of netzach is to break through as many barriers (klipot) as possible, which arise from gevurah's influence. This scenario is the basis of the imagery of conquest in the Torah, such as in the narrative of King David.

Relative circumstances are analyzed through netzach's counterpart—hod. Netzach expansively seeks to break through and explore. In turn, hod summarizes toward a conclusion by reduction. It excludes all extraneous possibilities to focus the expansive energy of netzach on specifics. Hod and netzach work cooperatively to allow the mind to engage phenomena with detailed precision.

Like netzach, hod is only a tool of intention. It can resonate in a powerful and open manner or it can become trapped in limited conceptual details. Hod is indispensable in mystical contemplation, where the mind needs to follow an undistracted path. It allows the mind to hold to subtle states that can become deeply refined. This justifies its name, which translates as "splendor." In the highest sense, hod resonates with the brilliance of the luminosity of basic space and becomes bitul to it, cutting through the infinite backwash of excess information that causes distraction.

Together, as the "gates of prophecy," hod and netzach insure that concentration can use energy effectively for spiritual inquiry. However, in a conventional sense, these sefirot are only tools of ordinary egoic identification.

(1:20) Elohim said: "Let the waters teem with swarms of living creatures and let the birds fly above the earth in the open space of the heavens." (1:21) And thus Elohim created the great taninim (sea dwellers), and every living creature that creeps with which the waters teem, of its kind, and every winged bird of its kind, and Elohim saw that it was good. (Gen. 1:20–21)

The narrative of the fifth day expresses hod through the profusion of living creatures that fill the sea and sky. What the fourth day was to the differentiation of light, the fifth day is to the differentiation of living beings. The water creatures and birds refer to energetic patterns, which "come to life." The birds symbolize the angels (melekim), which manifest in the heavens. This usually pertains to the world of yetzirah, but overlaps with briah and assiah as well.

Angels are not autonomous entities with independent existence, of course. No being has independent existence, including human beings. Angels are energetic configurations that exert influence within the inner life of phenomena. They "fly" above the baseline of ordinary human perception and occasionally make encounters with it. The sea creatures refer to energetic patterns that dwell beneath human awareness, mixing within its subconscious recesses. Both classes of creatures express a functional specificity that differentiates them, thus they are related to hod and appear on the fifth day.

It is important to realize that neither the birds nor the sea creatures are aspects of the "human" mind in a psychologized sense. They are aspects of Ain Sof's creative diversity, which is the animating power that all modes of being express. This is where kabbalah departs from Jungian theory. Jung postulated that archetypes "bubble up" from the collective unconscious, the great cosmic repository of creative axioms. From the kabbalistic standpoint this is narcissism, because the collective begins and ends with the projection of human conceptual hopes and fears. Human beings attempt to "own" whatever phenomenon is encountered, whether consciously or subconsciously. True gnostic wisdom is revealed from beyond conceptuality and its archetypes, and enters the human realm as a portal. On the other side are not the root patterns of conceptuality, as Jung believed, but the capacity to nullify self-identification altogether.

Human cognitive patterns resonate inexorably with living patterns of infinite types. The link between the realms is interwoven. The "birds" and "sea creatures" typify a wide range of nonhuman forms that are encountered in mystical ascent. Often these beings appear in anthropomorphic guise, which the human mind projects in order to perceive and communicate effectively. The *Zohar* refers to this:

> "Let the waters swarm with living souls:" these are the lower waters teeming with varieties as above. Those higher, these lower . . . "And let birds fly upon the earth," messengers from above appearing to

human beings in human appearance, as implied by the words "fly upon the earth." There are others who appear only in the ruach according to human awareness. (*Zohar*)

As a unit, netzach and hod negotiate the interaction between heaven and earth. They are called the "wheels of the chariot" because they motivate the zivug of Zer Anpin and Nukva toward or away from consummation. In order to understand this, the image of the chariot must be examined. It is one of the most important images in all of Jewish mysticism.

The Divine chariot or *merkavah* has many profound variations of meaning. This term dates back to the temple period, and is synonymous with that stage of early Jewish mysticism. A merkavah both moves and houses creativity. Like all phenomena, its motion appears to the human mind within the bi-directional process of "running and returning." This terminology evolved an aspect of the tradition that predates kabbalah as we know it today. It is rooted in the first chapter of Ezekiel where the symbol of the merkavah itself is described. This will be discussed more fully later.

Generally speaking, the merkavah "descends" into appearance and "ascends" as the realization of its nature, reflecting the complete scope of the Shechinah's display of phenomena. However, the term *merkavah* is specifically related to human adaptation and mastery over that process. It is human mystical accomplishment that makes the merkavah move to reveal whatever it reveals. The merkavah is a structural mirror of the mind that rides it. It is guided by "brains," which is KaChaB (keter, chochmah, binah). The potential of the brain is executed by its "body," which is the lower seven sefirot. It has four stages that correspond to the four worlds, which in turn express the tenfold array. The merkavah is the master pattern inherent in whatever the mind manifests.

To sum this up, the merkavah itself, the ten sefirot, and the four letters of the Divine Name are all synonymous. Linking these aspects of the structure of creativity is the real meaning of the Divine Image diagram. The synergy between the ten sefirot and four letters of YHVH constitutes one grand merkavah, which can be applied to any form of expression. The merkavah is revealed on both microcosmic and macrocosmic levels. This distinction is pure dualism, as these categories are completely interdependent. In order to accept that a world exists, a being would have to exist in that world and perceive it. In order to accept that a being exists, it would have to appear somewhere, which would require a world. The break from this logic is radical unity and the nullification of the self-identification that allows dualism to operate. If mind realizes its nature, it no longer distinguishes between itself and its realm. However, it will not accept or reject the appearance of either, simply because the apparition of beings and worlds present themselves to the mind. The tzaddikim teach us that phenomena appear beyond reality and unreality, self and other, and can be engaged without dualistic grasping.

In the process of this realization ripening, the merkavah appears to move through worlds. Human beings try to understand all of these phenomena dualistically. On the level of assiah, the merkavah manifests the individual human body as well as the whole physical realm. On the level of yetzirah, motion manifests both "internal" perception as well as "external" energy, which is felt and thought about. On the level of briah, the axiomatic potential of basic space manifests as the human capacity for thought, as well as the open possibility of all "outside" ideas that can be encountered and learned. However, on the level of atzilut, microcosmic and macrocosmic applications can no longer be distinguished, as they are manifested as an undifferentiated luminous potential. The intention of the mystic is to nullify all three worlds to their common nature so that none continue to be divided. Only when all worlds and all perception of worlds become bitul can the true nature of the merkavah be realized.

The "wheels" of the merkavah interface between energy and apparitional space, where perceptual conditions gel into a coherent form. This takes place as the triad NeHiY becomes the catalyst for the interaction of tiferet and malkut. This is referred to in the thirteenth-century text *Sefer HaIyyun:*

> Below the curtain revolving in the revolution of its brilliance, before the powers mentioned, there are the wheels of the merkavah, which are the catalysts of the heavens. (*Sefer HaIyyun*)

As stated, the wheels of the merkavah are moved by intention, which determines where the merkavah goes and what it becomes. The merkavah can be a vehicle to aspire toward freedom and struggle against obstacles. It can also enter the labyrinth of confusion in which mind becomes imprisoned. The human mind can be trapped in the mire that manifests between tiferet and malkut, which occultists naively refer to as the "astral plane." It is like a barrier that arises between heaven and earth. In the quote a "curtain" is mentioned beyond the merkavah's wheels. This refers to the barrier of conventional perception, which usually blocks the pure energy of upper yetzirah (ChaGaT) from view. Below this curtain the dull cycle of conventional interactions between NeHiY and malkut persist, and zivug cannot be realized. Beyond this is a "revolution of brilliance," the visionary scope of phenomena. Ordinary perception is blind to its subtle expression.

DAY 6

The sixth day of creation is represented by the sefirah of yesod. Yesod is the point of integration between the six aspects of energy and the space of appearance. It is here that the zivug of Zer Anpin and the Shechinah is consummated. Netzach and hod may shape the bond between heaven and earth, but no matter what they do, their endeavors will always converge at yesod. As stated, their collective triad is known by the acronym NeHiY (netzach, hod, yesod). In a cognitive sense, this represents the lower half of the complete ruach: the sixfold complex of energetic motion that constitutes the perceptual scope of a human being.

Yesod regulates modes of cognition. The degree of integration that is determined by yesod becomes galvanized into mental pictures, feelings, and concepts, which human beings call their "reality." Conventionally, this makes yesod the "seat of personal consciousness." In a nonconventional sense yesod is a Divine wedding, continually celebrated by the tzaddikim.

When covered by klipah-barriers, yesod functions as the ego: the false sense of independent existence. When unfettered by klipot, the ego is rendered bitul, and yesod becomes an open portal. This must be thoroughly understood. There is no tangible "soul" or "self" to be set free within the human experience. The degree to which the illusion of individual autonomy is nullified depends on how thoroughly self-fixated habit patterns are dissolved. When these habits dissolve they simply disappear into pregnant space, which ironically is equal to the nature of the mind they conceal. Neither has any solid reality in an objective sense. Habits are only sustained by the "food" of attention. The constrictive klipot that reify them can be metaphorically starved by changing the way that attention is utilized. When there is no more fixation on a subject and an object the mind simply abides as the open expanse of its essential nature, which is limitless Ain Sof.

When reifying habits begin to slip away, the mind's cognitive picture slowly begins to unfold into vast substanceless luminosity, and its vivid beauty shines as endless visionary self-ornamentation. This "cleansing of the lens" of yesod defines our spiritual state, and is the key to determining the actual condition the mind manifests.

Without egocentric habits, the ruach is free to run and return without obstruction. This manifests the unceasing energy of the visionary paradise known as "Eden." To a tzaddik there is nothing but the perfect unity of primordial seed and womb. It is for this reason that all tzaddikim are said to have "perfected" yesod, where the opportunity for gnosis in all its fullness is actualized. In this sense they have realized the common basis of all phenomena. This is implied by the literal meaning of the word yesod, which is foundation. Through this we can understand the famous phrase: "The tzaddik is the *foundation* of the world."

Considering the language of the "mature" or "immature" zivug can be problematic. When kabbalists refer to the zivug as "incomplete" this must be understood only as a metaphor for the deceptions of ordinary cognition. It is the state of a person's habits that are "incomplete." The imagery of marital dysfunction describes the inability of beings to realize the interdependent bond of motion and space, within which neither has any independent reality. This means that the bliss of their wedding is open, intangible, and free. Instead of visionary freedom, ordinary beings generally perceive conflict, fragmentation, and entropy. Both views are sealed by the status of yesod.

From the point of view of faith, the zivug of Zer Anpin and Nukva is unceasingly consummated without interruption. These *partufim* (personifications of the sefirot) are always in union. The zivug of phenomenal energy and apparitional space is always perfect, whole, and pure, reflecting the primordial union of chochmah and binah. Holding to this primordial purity as the nature of phenomena is the essence of faith and the basis of the mystical view.

> Elohim said: "Let the earth bring forth living creatures, each of its kind, domesticated animals, creeping things, and beasts of the earth, each of its kind." (Gen. 1:24)

The narrative of the sixth day begins with the creation of the land animals. This picks up where the fifth day left off. The fifth day was concerned with the creatures of water and sky: the influences that manifest above and below the immanent cognitive space of human beings. The sixth day articulates how living forms manifest on the earth itself, which is the central space of manifestation. The sky and sea are peripheral realms that are indirect in their implications. Day six is the culmination of the whole scope, the entire field of Shechinah.

Life manifesting upon the earth recalls the third day. On the third day the earth is *seen* and the harmony of vision established. Yesod is the culmination of that sixfold activity, which links directly with the space of malkut. Therefore, tiferet and yesod are two ends of a continuum. Yesod consummates the marriage that tiferet proposes. This is hinted at by the fact that yesod is attributed to the sixth day, an echo of tiferet which is the sixth sefirah. The *Zohar* symbolically articulates their relationship within the context of the larger picture:

> The waters flow from above, from the upper heh. Under the heavens is a "small vav." So there is "vav-vav": one is heaven, the other is under heaven. "Let dry land appear" is the final heh. (*Zohar*)

From basic space (upper *heh*) the *vav* of tiferet (heaven) emerges. Yesod seals its function through a "small *vav*" beneath it, which establishes contact with malkut. Between them creativity runs and returns. The small *vav* indicates the sub-gap within the heavens of the triad NeHiY, which is where conventional dualism or "double vision" easily takes hold. This is symbolized by the doubling of the *vav*s. The two *vav*s are utilized in the four expansions of the name YHVH, whose sums are 72, 63, 45, and 52. In all four configurations each *vav* is doubled. The *vav*s represent the triads of ChaGaT and NeHiY, which the *Zohar* calls "heaven and under heaven." Thus "*vav-vav*" represents the whole structure of the ruach. Through its integration with the final *heh*, "dry land" is established and the appearance of cohesive form is manifested.

Yesod corresponds to the genitals in the symbolism of the human body. There biological reproduction is sealed. As a mirror of the union of the supernal parents, the lower union emerges as the key to gnosis. As stated earlier, the womb of the *heh* is co-emergent with the seed of its impregnation, representing a whole "self-manifesting" creativity. It is not born into existence; it only reflects its nature into the blissful play of luminosity and space, which is manifested as the dance of energy and its contextual space. Since this realization largely depends on yesod, it becomes the pivot to apprehend the greater wholeness, which is gnosis itself.

This is why on the sixth day the Divine Image is explicitly recognized in the biblical narrative. It arises through the vision of yesod in the most important verse of the entire first chapter: 1:26. There the merkavah of human life is articulated to reflect Divinity:

Elohim said: "Let us make man in our image and likeness."
(Gen. 1:26)

First, consider the number of verse 26. This is the gematria of the name YHVH: Yud (10) + Heh (5) + Vav (6) + Heh (5) = 26. In verse 1:26 the vision of all of the patterns that articulate the grand scope of creativity can be linked: the four letters YHVH, the ten sefirot, and the structure of the human form. This should be evident through the Divine Image diagram that depicts them integrated as a standing merkavah. The inner symbolism of the merkavah can be applied to the creative process in every aspect of manifestation. This is the central correspondence of this commentary, and the blueprint for all phenomena. It also will be the key to the symbolic narrative of Eden in the second and third chapters.

As previously mentioned, the term *merkavah* is associated with Ezekiel's vision of a four-stage Divine chariot. Each of the stages represents one of the letters of YHVH. The image symbolizes the ascent of the mind through the projection of its worlds, and is the purest Jewish symbol for what a mystical practitioner actually engages in.

At the apex of Ezekiel's description of the merkavah is a human form. This is the culmination of its function and meaning. This apex reflects the complete Divine Image, and is literally the "driving force" that guides the fourfold mechanism. Both the chariot and this "driver" are representations of the same pattern, which is the pattern of the merkavah and the sefirot. The verse number is extremely significant—it is verse 26 of Ezekiel's first chapter. Thus Ezekiel 1:26 reflects the same image as Genesis 1:26. Here are the texts:

> Above the space [rakia] that was over their heads, like a vision of sapphire, was the form of a throne, and over the form of the throne there was a form like a vision of a man upon it from above. (Ezekiel 1:26)

And:

> Elohim said: "Let us make man in our image and likeness." And thus Elohim created man in his image. In the image of Elohim he created him, male and female he created them. (Gen. 1:26–27)

The phrase: "In the image of Elohim" suggests that the human image is a direct reflection of the Shechinah. Associating the Divine Image to Elohim reflects binah, the essential heart-space of manifestation. The creativity inherent in this image manifests through the variation of interdependent contrasts. The mirror that is the basis of all of these reflections is the Shechinah, which is the presence of the nature of Ain Sof. This is why the texts suggest that Elohim offers the image of YHVH.

The infinite variation of the Shechinah is hinted at with the contrast between verse 1:26, which states: "In the Image he created *him*," and verse 1:27 which states: "male and female he created *them*." The plural form represents the infinite application of the reflections of the master pattern, which is the function of the pregnant space of Elohim.

In the Divine Image diagram yesod falls in the center of the horizontal window of the lower *heh*. It occupies the lowest spot in the ruach. The highest spot is at daat, at the center of the horizontal of the upper *heh*. Daat is not one of the ten sefirot, nor is it an eleventh sefirah. It is a synthesis of keter, chochmah, and binah that emerges to engage the lower seven sefirot. It is the bridge between the two upper worlds (*yud-heh*) and the two lower worlds (*vav-heh*). Daat allows the supernal nature to become integrated with the phenomena of "the days." This is similar to what yesod does within these days. Yesod creates the stability that allows daat's greater unity to become evident within phenomena. Between daat and yesod the waters become bitul to each other; energetic reflections run and return in infinite echoes throughout primordial space.

The perfection of yesod depends upon the brit (circumcision). If we disregard the religious physical application of this (which has no apparent gnostic function), then the act perfectly symbolizes the purification of egoic klipot. When yesod is free of obscurations the union of luminosity and space shines clearly from keter to malkut, and Ain Sof's tzimtzum offer only pure apparitional play no matter what appears.

Since the zivug of the lower worlds is necessary to reveal the primordial union of chochmah and binah, it is up to yesod to establish the requisite conditions. Because of this crucial role, yesod is referred to as "lower daat." This is evident in the Bible when sexual union is described as daat, as in: "The man *knew* his wife" (daat literally means "knowing"). The ultimate conclusion of daat—which corresponds with the primordial Ruach Elohim—comes when yesod establishes complete phenomenal integration. Yesod's purity is the realization that *all appearances are equal to Ruach Elohim*. When the tzimtzumim of the ruach are made bitul, the primordial status of "before creation" literally "sings" through the six days, and the Garden of Eden is uncovered, as we will see.

Within the Divine Image diagram "water-water" is nullified when the ruach is fully expanded from daat to yesod. This is the state of gadlut (expanded consciousness). When yesod and daat are harmonized, tiferet reveals its complete *kavod* (glory). This expanded scope makes NeHiY and ChaGaT into a stable and complete spectrum that holds all phenomena as "the rainbow of song." This state is known as Ruach Ha-Kodesh (Holy ruach), as mentioned earlier, which is one of the many titles for prophecy. Prophecy is gnosis: the capacity to know the essential nature of all circumstance directly. It is not the ability to predict future events, although divinatory powers and foresight might accompany the gnosis of some tzaddikim, as well as many other special powers.

The theme of the remaining narrative of the sixth day is man's domination of the world's appearances. Of course this is a topic ripe for abuse by religious fundamentalists, which hardly needs comment. What human beings dominate in spiritual life is the mistaken notion of a separate subject self experiencing a world of separate unrelated objects. By cultivating Ruach Ha-Kodesh, human beings master the integration of energy and space in the cognitive process. This is illustrated by the repetition of two of the three aspects of energetic manifestation described on the third day: seed-bearing herbs and trees that have seed-bearing fruit. The grasses are excluded to show that human life differs from the grass-feeding animals because humans are mostly defined by participation in larger cycles and patterns, which hold out the potential to be mastered. The text states:

> (1:28) Elohim blessed them, and Elohim said to them: "Be fruitful and multiply, fill the earth and subdue it, and dominate the fish of the sea, the birds of the heaven, and every creeping thing that moves upon the earth." (1:29) Elohim said: "Behold I have given you all seed bearing herbs that are on the surface of the earth, and every tree that has seed bearing fruit, to you it shall be for food. (1:30) And for every animal of the earth, for every bird of the heaven, and for everything that creeps on the ground in which there is a living nefesh soul, all herbs shall be their food." And it became so. (1:31) Elohim saw all that he had made and behold it was very good. It was evening and morning, day six. (Gen. 1:28–31)

PART II

PRIMORDIAL GNOSIS AND ITS OBSCURATION

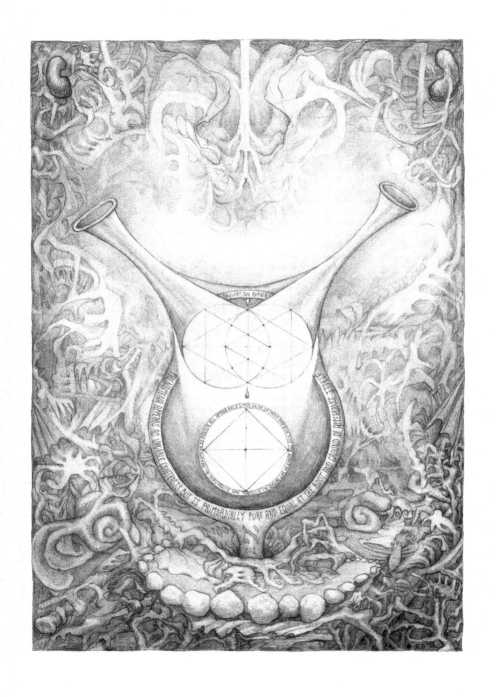

REIFICATION REPAIR

THE PHENOMENA APPEARS AS VARIABLE CONTRASTS BUT IS PRIMORDIALLY PURE AND EQUAL AT THE ROOT AND GROUND OF APPEARANCE ITSELF

3

THE EDÉNIC STATE

Commentary on the
Second Chapter of Genesis

The first chapter ends with the most important image of the entire
Bible: the merkavah of the Divine Image. However, the blueprint
of the creative process is not yet complete. The seventh day, corresponding to the sefirah of malkut, has yet to be described. Malkut
is not included in the first chapter because it relates directly to the
central theme of the second: the Garden of Eden. It has been clearly
established that malkut is not separate in any way from the primordial space of binah. Within this space the activity of the six days
cease, and are declared "Holy." It is from the holiness of this essential
nature that the Garden of Eden arises. Therefore the second chapter
begins with the basic space of creation functioning as the ground
of all phenomena and variation. With this understanding as a base
the rest of the chapter will unfold to describe the Divine nature of
perception.

> (2:1) The heavens and the earth were completed, and so were all
> their conglomerations. (2:2) Elohim completed by the seventh day
> all the work which he had made, and he abstained on the seventh
> day from all his work which he had made. (2:3) Elohim blessed the

seventh day and declared it to be Holy, for on it He abstained from all his work, which Elohim had created. (Gen. 2:1–3)

The cessation of activity symbolizes the vast expanse of space at the heart of all motion. The narrative suggests that on the seventh day the womb of primordial space asserts its omnipresence, and the six days are all bitul to it. This day of "rest" is no mere empty void in which motion is placed on hold. It portrays the open dynamism of space that is the secret life of the six days. This aspect comes to full bloom in the Garden of Eden, which allows pregnant space to reveal infinite beauty.

Malkut's space reveals its open and fertile nature by accepting and adapting to whatever the six aspects of motion do. Through "resting" in the seventh day the six days "return" back to the same primordial space from which they arose. Nothing ever leaves the basic space of the Shechinah. There is nowhere to go to or come from. The Shechinah's nature nullifies the mistaken notion that malkut and binah are the "beginning" and "end" of a linear process.

Ten sefirot of nothingness: Their end is imbedded in their beginning, and their beginning in their end, like a flame and a burning coal. (*Sefer Yetzirah*)

Cosmic creativity is bitul to the vast expanse of Ain Sof. Still, every possible form and sensation arise. This is the inherent paradox of the Shechinah, which "speaks" without ever breaking the primordial silence of its nature. It is upon this basis that Eden unfolds.

This is the history of the heaven and the earth when they were created on the day that YHVH ELOHIM made earth and heaven. (Gen. 2:4)

Verse 2:4 presents the continuum of the lower seven sefirot from two perspectives that "run and return." First the phrase "the heaven and the earth" is given, followed by "earth and heaven." This sequence addresses the manner in which energy functions. Understanding this must be comprehended before any consideration of gnosis or delusion begins. The words of this line ascend and descend, just as phenomena manifest and dissolve. The mind seeks to know and then retreats to rest in some mode of knowing. In conventional perception, this oscillating activity appears to go out from a fictitious "self" to meet the thoughts, feelings, or objects that it comprehends. However, from the view of radical unity, there are no such origins or destinations. Divine equality is locationless and ubiquitous to infinite space.

The sequence of this verse illustrates two directions. The first ordering (the heaven and the earth) suggests the descent into manifestation, as presented in the first chapter. The second ordering (earth and heaven) suggests the opposing direction, which is malkut ascending back upward. The verse is like a mirror that reflects creativity to itself. The first order suggests the process of becoming, the second suggests the struggle of adaptation that seeks to realize the Divine nature or gets stuck at some point along the way. This oscillation between them alludes to the mirrorlike aspect of mind itself, which reflects phenomena according to habit. Gnosis is the equality of these directions in which they are recognized as bitul to each other. In such a state the words that divide their differences lose all relative meaning. In the gnostic state, the running and returning of energy reveals the ultimate clarity of the mirror of the Shechinah without any obscuration whatsoever.

The relationship between the directions is reminiscent of a famous line from *The Emerald Tablet of Hermes*, a major Hermetic alchemical tract, reputedly of ancient origin:

That which is below is like that which is above, and that which is above is like that which is below. By this miracle the accomplishment of One Thing is realized. (*The Emerald Tablet of Hermes*)

From the perspective of gnosis, manifestation is the glory of the Shechinah. This is indicated by the addition of the letter *heh* with the words "*the* heaven and *the* earth" in the first ordering. A *heh* is used as a prefix to indicate a definite article (*the* earth), thus it is "*Ha*-aretz" instead of just "aretz" (the same holds for the word for "heaven," which is *Ha*-Shemayim). This renders it "*the* heaven and *the* earth."

The *heh*s in this first ordering indicate that the heart of the Shechinah's presence is the primordial basis of phenomena. In the second ordering there is a tendency for this to become obscured. The absence of *heh*s in the second ordering (earth and heaven) reminds us that the returning ascent is most often flawed by belief in separate appearances that lose sight of mother space. Before any understanding of the Edenic state can commence, the actual condition of human beings must be acknowledged. This is symbolized by the "loss" of the *heh* in the ascent back toward the Divine nature. Based on an understanding of this loss further refinement can be approached.

In verse 2:4 the Divine Name changes from Elohim, which was used exclusively in the first chapter, to YHVH Elohim. This is of crucial importance. This compound name will be used throughout the second and third chapters. It represents a shift from articulating the blueprint of creativity to an exposition of the fruit of that process.

On one level, the names YHVH and Elohim pose a contrast. YHVH represents the "giving" of creative opportunity associated with the right side. Elohim represents the contextuality of space that structures that creativity and is attributed to the left side. Therefore the composite name YHVH Elohim indicates a harmony, which consists of an interdependence between the sides. This is an indication of Eden's inner disposition. Eden's structural variation directly reveals its essential nature, and does so without conflict. From this point onward the narrative will express this harmonious perfection, until it becomes apparent that its unity actually includes imperfection. This harsh realization will be the subject of the third chapter.

All the plants of the field were not yet upon the earth, and all the herbal vegetation of the field had not yet sprouted, for YHVH ELOHIM had not brought rain upon the earth, and there was no Adam (human) to work the adamah (soil). (Gen. 2:5)

Verse 2:5 begins the narrative that actually describes Eden. The first chapter rendered a structural vision of creativity, based on the correspondences of the sefirot. Both second and third chapters apply this structure to an allegorical account of cognition and its phenomena. In this account the sefirot's pristine order will be turned inside out to ask the question of what mind's function really is.

The narrative begins with the temporal metaphor of a state "before" the plants of the field had sprouted. This is a window beyond time into the primordial state of the Shechinah. It corresponds with primordial daat and its Ruach Elohim, which is pregnant with the potential to generate creative specificity. As an undifferentiated potentiality, it represents the condition "before" perception becomes defined in any way by concepts or mental constructs.

The perspective of daat allows a bird's-eye view from which to contemplate the forthcoming imagery. What is seen through this portal is a series of extremely dense symbols with many layers of meaning. First, the "field" in which the plants will grow is the field of perception. It is comprised of the middle six sefirot and malkut together, but the emphasis is on the Shechinah's space from which the whole field manifests. Its "plants" are the six aspects of cognitive movement, which differentiate the basic space of the field.

The plants can only flourish if the field has proper nourishment. The only true nourishment is unceasing awareness of its essential nature, which comes from beyond superficial circumstance. This nourishment takes the form of the need for rain from the upper waters, which is suggested in relation to human effort. The implied connection between the rain and "man to work the soil" is at the very heart of this commentary. The world that human beings know is the direct result of mind's labor. The undifferentiated potential of Ain Sof arises as a universe of diverse appearances only through the active motion of perception. This work "below" brings rain from "above." This relationship must be understood for the rest of the chapter's points to make any sense at all.

The water that sustains the field is the bounty of spiritual potential called *shefa* (blessing force). It is the lifeblood of creative activity, the fluid continuity of the upper waters of the supernal triad, which directly empowers the appearances of malkut. Verse 2:5 states that the rain is "brought from YHVH ELOHIM," but obliquely implies that this is dependent upon human behavior. In order to penetrate this relationship, what is meant by "human" in the first place must be examined.

The word for human life in its essential form is *Adam* (ADaM). Despite popular misconceptions, Adam is not an individual male human being or a collectivization of humanity in the Jungian sense. Adam is the pivot between boundless cognitive potential and the mind's temporary limitations. Adam is an open question. He is the opportunity to express the merkavah of the Divine Image. However, the question remains as to whether he will realize the fullness of his essential nature or succumb to the habits that obscure it. Adam's value in the Edenic metaphor is primarily this, which makes any preoccupation with Jungian archetype or individual versus collective identity decidedly irrelevant by comparison.

Adam's kabbalistic structure is complex. Although Adam embodies the complete Divine Image, his focus is centered in the world of *yetzirah* (tiferet). This is the fundamental context of the Edenic expression. The primary aspects that express Adam, at least at this point, are the six sefirot of the ruach. His work is the cultivation of gnosis, which is symbolized by bringing shefa into the earth. Thus Adam's role is to provide for malkut, and in so doing the upper and lower waters become unified.

Malkut's reception of shefa is actually part of Adam. Adam "contains" malkut, and thus represents all of manifestation. We will see that the relationship between Adam's six primary sefirot and malkut changes later in the chapter when his wife is taken from within Adam's body. This illustrates that she is there in him already, always has been and always will be. Malkut will emerge with the name "Eve" at the end of the third chapter. However, at this point she abides as a latent aspect within Adam until the time comes when the two aspects will be examined in relation to each other and their relationship becomes the main issue. Now the focus is on cognitive potential itself, not the relationships that extend from it. Remember, the point of view for this stage of chapter two is that of daat, which holds the seven sefirot of manifestation from the vantage point of the Ruach Elohim.

Malkut's inherent connection with binah is expressed by the earth's need for the nourishment of water. Adam represents the potential to link above and below, and reveal the wholeness of things. His central position expresses the inner meaning of Eden, which views all phenomena from the standpoint of pure gnostic potential. If this is understood, it should be clear that Eden is an aspect of Adam himself. He is the link that allows all the symbols mentioned thus far to be included in a single great merkavah.

What follows in verse 2:6 alters the structure of the imagery that has been previously examined. The impending rain's nourishment of the ground is provided in a most unexpected way—it comes *up* from the ground rather than down from above—it rises as "mist." This distinction marks a major shift. It leads the reader to expect a linear relationship between above and below. It informs the reader that *above is already below,* and it simply asserts itself outright. This transition point invites the reader into the Edenic vision on its own terms, which is the visionary display of the world of yetziric energy.

> A mist rose up from the earth, and it watered the entire surface of the adamah. (Gen. 2:6)

The image of the self-watering ground is very potent. It reinforces that the source of shefa is actually a-directional and beyond the reference points of conceptual logic. The source of shefa is omnipresent Shechinah. Contemplating this breaks the rigid separation between above and below that is the most common line of division between god and creation in exoteric symbology. Through the self-watering ground of appearance the Shechinah arises as the simultaneity of both upper and lower waters. It is water itself, as opposed to "water-water." This simultaneity is equal with unborn B'reshit. It can appear anywhere, everywhere, or nowhere, regardless of apparent divisions.

The primordial self-watering earth supports the sixfold "plant growth" of the Edenic state. Understanding the implications of the symbol of earth is a key to the whole Edenic allegory. The Hebrew word for the soil or ground upon which the plants depend is *adamah*. The adamah is literally "the ground of phenomena." Coming to know (or ignore) this ground is the catalytic factor that determines whether human beings become nihilistic materialists, oblivious consumers, religious dilettantes, aspiring contemplative mystics, or simple interested parties. This realization also governs whether the world is taken as random, fragmented bits of material or as the magical play of Ain Sof—a product of how the adamah "waters" perception.

The word adamah includes the name of Adam with a *heh* added on the end. Thus it can be read as *Adam-Heh* (ADaM-aH). This incorporates both perceptual motion and its apparitional display. It is the basis of the "field." It also illustrates Adam's role as both integral and equal to the display of the earth. The idea that consciousness is the key to the world's appearance is quite a radical idea by popular standards, even though Heidegger came pretty close to directly spelling this out almost a century ago. Regardless, the early Jewish mystics have held this view since before the Second Temple period, as texts such as *Sefer Yetzirah* prove.

Verse 2:6 precedes a major transition in the narrative. The adamah is being expressed from the viewpoint of daat, which is "before"

Adam actually appears in the narrative. This view holds consciousness as undifferentiated potential, and addresses Adam from a speculative point of view. The next verse begins a progression into cognitive differentiation, where Adam becomes active and performs.

Before this step is given, a review of the functions of a human being according to the kabbalists will be helpful. The five levels that articulate mind's modes of function are given below in greater detail, in anticipation of the forthcoming narrative:

LEVEL	SEFIRAH	FUNCTION
1. Yechidah	Keter	Unborn essence (*pure cognizant potentiality*)
2. Chayah	Chochmah	Dynamic nature (*pure knowingness*)
3. Neshamah	Binah	Axiomatic space (*the capacity for thought*)
4. Ruach	Middle Six	Perceptual movement (*activity of thinking and feeling*)
5. Nefesh	Malkut	Display of vital presence (*apparitional display*)

The last two levels make up the field of perception that is taken as the conventional "reality" of a human being. This consists of the ruach (the movement of the mind in the formation of thoughts and feelings) and the nefesh (the vital presence that is displayed as a result of movement). Ruach and nefesh together are referred to by their acronym: *NeR*. Ner also means "lamp," which is a means to express light. The symbolism should be obvious.

Beyond the scope of the NeR is *neshamah*. A person's neshamah is a great mystery. It is neither the person nor is it otherwise. The neshamah is fundamentally the open space of Shechinah, which is replete with all the wisdom of B'reshit. It can become anything, but when causes and conditions impose limitations due to habit, it is set within the boundaries of ordinary human life. Only great tzaddikim realize the wisdom that is inherent within the neshamah. From that basis the secrets of the highest levels are revealed. Without the obscuring limitations produced by egocentric habits, the mind is free.

An ordinary NeR is a product of habits cultivated over many lifetimes. There is no external god to blame. Each person makes his or her own reality and must take radical responsibility for it. Therefore habit is the main concern in spiritual growth. This is the central theme of the third chapter of Genesis where the obscuration of the Edenic state is described, which is nothing other than the habit of concealment.

The nefesh, ruach, and neshamah all yearn to freely express the light of Ain Sof, which is their essential nature. These three levels together are known by the acronym NaRaN (nefesh-ruach-neshamah). To a tzaddik NaRaN is bitul to Ain Sof. It is the conduit that shines the light of the two highest levels (keter/yechidah and chochmah/chayah) into the lives of others for their ultimate benefit. This is pure compassion. A tzaddik is nothing but this, as is suggested by Rebbe Nachman in the following excerpt:

> Know! There is a light higher than nefesh, ruach, and neshamah. It is the light of Ain Sof. And though the intellect cannot grasp it, the racing of the mind nevertheless pursues it. And by virtue of this racing, the intellect is able to grasp it in an aspect of "reaching and not reaching." For the truth is that it is not possible to grasp it because it is above nefesh, ruach, and neshamah. And know! It is impossible to even grasp it in the aspect of reaching and not reaching, except by performing good deeds with joy. (*Likutey Moharan*)

The subtlest levels of chayah and yechidah are undifferentiated aspects of the essential nature of Ain Sof, completely beyond thought and perception. Rebbe Nachman points out that this is nothing other than pure joy, which is the bliss of the mind's nature. Ordinary people know nothing of this, but we can feel its proximity in an oblique manner. It arises in our lives as the wish to be happy. What is happiness? Can it be anything other than knowing that the essence and nature of creativity is implicit in all phenomena? The central message of the Edenic allegory is that when perception does not obscure Divinity, *everything is bliss.* In fact, the word *Eden* itself means "delight."

We call Divinity "good" for no reason other than the fact that it expresses its nature. Its nature is radiant, creative, playful, and vivid. When they are not obscured through self-serving concerns and illusions, all phenomena are the Garden of Eden. This is the state of the tzaddik, and the question of Adam's fate. Even in the concentration camps with the torment of the Nazis coming down full force upon them, the tzaddikim that were imprisoned never strayed from the joy of the Divine. This is because their joy did not depend on any circumstance or condition; it is the nature of all conditions. This indestructible, intemporal, and intangible joy is literally the heart of the Shechinah that awaits recognition.

The next section marks another major shift. In verse 2:7 Adam is formed; he literally embodies the shefa-infused adamah. This is of critical importance—Adam is Shechinah incarnate. Now the vision shifts to the perspective of tiferet, which is Adam's focal point. This is an opportunity to study the Shechinah through the lens of tiferet, which is the key to the expression of its glory. This begins the study of the specifics of the cognitive process, symbolized by Adam's experience in Eden. It begins vividly in this verse:

YHVH ELOHIM formed the Adam from the dust of the adamah and blew into his nostrils the breath of life. And so Adam became a living soul (nefesh-chayah). (Gen. 2:7)

The display of Adam as the merkavah of the Divine Image is the core of the Edenic vision, and here it arises to assert itself. From here on all of the symbols in the narrative will be given from the standpoint of Adam's cognitive state, including the symbol of the earth and Eden itself.

In 2:7 it seems that the earth arises as Adam, but it is actually the other way around. Adam is the activity of mind's motion. He is the self-arising synergy between the adamah and the life-breath. He embodies the precious primordial water that suffuses the adamah, which is malkut's supernal basis. This wisdom water is the living power of B'reshit. Adam arises from the unification of two major symbols: the *watery earth* and the *breath of life*. Their interaction is male and female reproductive symbolism. The life breath functions as "seed" and the earth is the aspect of the "womb." Verse 2:7 places these elements in a vertical relationship: the seed enters from "above" and the womb receives it "below." However, womb and seed are co-emergent and inseparable. Their simultaneity is implicit. Holding this view allows the image to function non-dualistically.

The entry of the intangible potentiality of the breath into the open fertility of the earth is not what it seems to be. Despite literary appearances, this relationship transcends the ordinary linear cause-and-effect relationship. It represents continual autogenesis. To understand this properly, the essential nature of creativity at the heart of appearance must be honored. If its wisdom is appreciated, then this metaphor sings a song of simultaneity, and the marriage of breath and earth displays the boundless fertility of B'reshit. The usual kabbalistic correspondence is: life-breath is keter, earth is malkut, and Adam is tiferet, which unifies them. However, it is not that simple. Beyond correspondence is primordial creative tension in the heart of all contrasts. Adam personifies this fundamental tension, which is the basis of cognitive motion. It assumes its qualities through the activity of running and returning. It descends from "the heaven to the earth" and ascends as "earth to heaven."

On a deeper level, the life-breath presents the seminal aspect of the *yud,* which initiates and catalyzes growth, and the earth is its corresponding aspect of *heh*. Together they project the living "blood of space" inherent in all contextual variation. Their common essence is represented by the upper point of the *yud*, from which every Hebrew letter is derived (graphically seen in each letter's upper left). The breath of life expands the "original point" and presents an opportunity to look into Ain Sof directly. It is synonymous with the avira, the essential luminous space mentioned in the *Zohar*. The avira is the basis of both space and light. The *Zohar*'s mention of it is an account from the level of keter:

> Ain Sof bursts out of itself as the avira, revealing the point of yud. Once this yud expands what remained was light (aur) from the mystery of the concealed avira. (*Zohar*)

The word *avira* is often translated as air, atmosphere, glow, or "aura." In Aramaic the word is spelled *alef-vav-yud-resh*. These letters spell out the word aur (light) with a *yud* left over (AVYR = AVR + Y). The *Zohar*'s equation implies that there is an essence-to-nature relationship between the avira and its radiant luminosity. The avira corresponds to keter, the "original point" of the *yud*, which radiates its luminous nature (chochmah). Avira then is seen as a keter-to-chochmah relationship: *yud* + *aur*. As the *Zohar* implies, avira is essentially the pure potentiality of Ain Sof, which is the root of both light and space. Avira is the whole *yud*, which is the root of both supernal parents. This is seen as *yud* conceals *heh* within its letter name (YVD: V + D = H with a Y left over for its self-impregnation).

In human terms, avira is pure unconditioned awareness that shines its pristine wisdom as all possible contexts, including those that obscure and obstruct it. It is a perfect unity that includes the possibility of imperfection (from a conventional standpoint). This is yet another hint at the content of the third chapter's inner meaning. We can further understand avira through a very important thirteenth-century text called *The Fountain of Chochmah:*

Before all of it there was avira, which is the root principle. From it emerged light, more refined than a thousand thousands thousands and ten thousand myriads of varieties of light. This is the primordial avira (avir kadmon), the root principle. Accordingly, it is called the Holy breath. (*The Fountain of Chochmah*)

The avira expresses light in the same way that the adamah is self-watering. The point that the self-watering ground emphasizes is that all phenomena are equally pregnant with possibility. These symbols are not limited by the logic of temporal motion. They display wholeness from the outset. Adam is not the "consequence" of the avira finding the earth. He is the self-arising display of its self-watering nature. If this metaphor becomes reduced to an ordinary mechanical process, then the subtlety of these potent mystical symbols is lost.

All reproductive contrasts are represented by the letter *bet* of the word B'reshit. The numerical value of the *bet* is two, which symbolizes male and female interactive polarity. The two partners are a unity beyond extremes, thus the number two represents apparitional paradox. This is also reflected in the esoteric meaning of *bet,* which is "house." In the conventional sense, a house is a container. It separates what is in it from whatever is outside of it. Adam embodies the basic space of the Shechinah, which is beyond containment, although everything that appears contained appears within it. All constructs—which contain and which are contained—are equally pregnant space themselves. Space appears as endless chains of containment, but its nature is beyond all appearances. The apparitional light inherent within space is co-emergent with it. This is the essence of the "two," which is the "house" in which the alchemical marriage takes place. The *bet* of B'reshit represents the paradox "in" which the continual reshit-beginning manifests. This is doubly reinforced, since reshit corresponds to chochmah, which is sefirah number two.

*

Adam is the house that explodes beyond the human dream of containment. He is human gnostic potential. Arising as the simultaneity of the self-watering adamah, Adam is what houses as well as what is housed, and as such, he represents what is free. In this sense Adam is Eden. The world arises according to what mind perceives. The *Zohar* suggests this with the image of the silkworm, whose body secretes a substance that becomes its own housing cocoon:

> Radiance sowing seed for its own glory, like the seed of fine purple silk wrapping itself within, weaving itself a palace. (*Zohar*)

Adam's role as tiferet expresses the all-embracing harmony of the span between malkut and keter. This bridge to the wholeness of the Divine Image is where perception can lead. The narrative invites human beings to see ourselves in this position. Intellectual understanding of gnosis is the first step, but ultimately perception itself will challenge us with disparities that are not theoretical. Cognition must be engaged to reveal its nature. This is what happens in the narrative. Adam's gnostic potential will be challenged in this way in the next part of the chapter.

The zivug of *vav* and *heh* is a stainless mirror that reflects the primordial purity of *yud-heh*. This is why Adam's forthcoming relationship with Eve will be so crucial. If the complete expression of YHVH is actualized, the mind becomes a merkavah of the full flowering of Ain Sof. In this sense the essential nature of mind is synonymous with its gnosis. Adam is the pivot between wholeness and fragmentation. This is the nature of human creative free will and its power of choice. To actualize its sublime nature in a living manner, gnosis must encompass the whole of life from its earthy facticity to its primordial essentiality. There is no escapist fantasy here; we are not whisked away from the daily toil to bypass suffering. Gnosis dawns within in the very phenomena that beings fixate upon and suffer through. The upper waters cannot be extracted from the reflections of the lower waters. Eluding the fallacy of "water-water" requires a complete merkavah. Understanding this gives the human experience its nobility and value. The ultimate opportunity of human growth is the synergy between the mind and the appearances of physical space, which is analogous to the synergy between life-breath and adamah.

> YHVH ELOHIM planted a garden in Eden, to the east, and there he placed the Adam he had formed. (Gen. 2:8)

In verse 2:8 the image of the garden emerges. Adam and his context are of an equal nature and cannot be separated, but they appear separate in the narrative for a reason. They articulate how the theater of perception operates: phenomenal reflections take on outer and inner roles in life; they assert a central unity in the gnosis of zivug, which will be brought out in two stages. The first is symbolized by Adam's relationship with the garden and its contents, the second will be symbolized by his relationship with his wife. These stages will attempt to consummate the zivug in various ways, but each will be met with obstacles that reflect human conceptual habits, which prevent gnosis. This will be evident in the third chapter.

The Edenic zivug is reflected in the name "Garden of Eden." The name has two parts: "Eden" corresponds with tiferet and "Garden" corresponds with malkut. As stated, Eden is synonymous with Adam himself and his focus at tiferet. The garden aspect is implicit within him for the time being (as his vital presence), but it will finally emerge to face him. Adam's Edenic state is only potential until the test of cognition alchemically puts it "through the fire" of actual perception. As mirror reflections of the same primordial essentiality, Adam's interaction with his garden will present the basic question: what will the mind do when it is faced with the prospect of phenomena that seem to be real and independent? Both aspects bear the consequences of the question.

Bringing malkut out to face Adam is the first stage of his maturation. This will be offered as his wife emerges for their zivug. At this point we should appreciate how these symbols reflect our own minds. The aspect of malkut is latent within Adam as he stands at the threshold of action. There are two possible directions it can take: gnosis or egoism. We all have the capacity for Edenic gnosis, but it is latent. It has to be brought out, cultivated, and realized or it remains a wasted opportunity. Recognizing the brilliant vividness of perception, by acknowledging the space that manifests it, is a stage in our own maturation.

The allegory of Eden is all about the ruach (creative and perceptual motion) and its relationship to its primordial nature. The question is whether a common basis emerges or whether the ruach devolves into chaos. The mind manifests its environment according to its disposition. Whatever external context a human being perceives is always a display of his or her spiritual and cognitive state. Who and what we are determines the kind of world we get. The state of Adam is the potential for Ruach Ha-Kodesh (Holy ruach). Until this point in the narrative malkut has posed no overt conflict. This will change in the last verses of the second chapter. Now the text will begin to prepare to face those harsh tendencies, which define human suffering and the habits that are its causes.

The garden inhabits the *eastern* direction. The designation of east corresponds to tiferet in kabbalistic literature, just as south is chesed, north is gevurah, west is yesod, above is netzach, and below is hod. The six directions elaborate tiferet's scope, as tiferet is sefirah number six and the *vav's* numerical value is six. This illustrates how Eden is the ultimate symbol of the pure realm of yetzirah: a state of energetic appearance that extends its essential nature. The Garden of Eden is synonymous with the capacity to manifest endless visions populated with endless forms of being. These dreamlike reflections are the domain of the ruach, a visionary realm of absolute beauty.

Artistic attempts to approximate the visionary state are abundant.

The Garden of Eden is synonymous with the imagination itself in much of Western art, where every conceivable image that can be wished for is made possible. Certainly the paintings of Hieronymus Bosch, many thirteenth- to sixteenth-century Italian paintings, and the works of the later surrealists come to mind to illustrate this.

The next series of verses mark another stage toward Adam's maturation. In order to understand it, verse 2:9 can be compared to a later group of verses (2:16–17). This will provide the scope with which to follow the leap that is forthcoming in the chapter.

> YHVH ELOHIM made grow from the adamah every tree that is pleasant to see and is good for food: the Tree of Life in the middle of the garden, and the Tree of Daat of Good and Evil. (Gen. 2:9)

And:

> (2:16) YHVH ELOHIM commanded the Adam saying: "You may certainly eat from every tree in the garden. (2:17) But from the Tree of Daat of what is Good and Evil you shall not eat from it, for on the day you eat from it you will certainly die." (Gen. 2:16–17)

With the verses between 2:9 and 2:17 we begin one of the most misunderstood and spiritually potent narratives in all of biblical literature. Before commencing, we should contemplate how our own actual condition contrasts the Edenic vision. The Garden of Eden represents the pristine state of cognitive perfection. This is the state our own minds would manifest spontaneously if it were not for the obscurations of our dualistic fixations. So few human beings have actually realized this that it is best to assume that we know next to nothing about it. Treating it as the most sublime of aspirations allows us to hold it in our hearts as the ultimate yearning and focus of our lives. This is the stance of the mystical practitioner. If we use the acknowledgment of our actual state to be the measure by which we decode these symbols, which portray true meaningfulness, then the text will become more to us than a mere intellectual interest. Then abiding in its words can become a real contemplative practice in its own right.

The inability to recognize and sustain the exalted state of Eden is the subject of the third chapter, but its roots are here in these verses of the second. This is precisely where exoteric religion loses its way, by making a series of errors that lead to some crucially destructive assumptions. This is also the point in the text where the gnostic content becomes most direct and explicit. It all depends on how a single symbol is interpreted in verse 2:17: the fruit of a tree that is forbidden for food.

Verse 2:9 states that the Tree of Life is situated in the *middle* of the garden. The attribution of the middle corresponds to the heart of the Edenic vision, which arises from the zivug union of luminous motion and space. Where then is the other tree, the Tree of Daat? Kabbalistic texts differ on this issue. Some attribute the Tree of Life to tiferet and the Tree of Daat to yesod. Others place the Tree of Daat peripherally to the two sides of the middle tree like a surrounding wall, as if the Tree of Daat represented the right and left sides, with the Tree of Life in between. All kabbalists proclaim that both trees are bound to a common root below the ground. This is because the adamah is unity itself. However, there is a clear division between its forms of "growth." Both unity and chaos are possible vectors for perception. Thus the conclusion must be made that the Tree of Daat is decidedly not in the middle of the garden where the Tree of Life is.

Moving forward to verse 2:17, a clear edict against eating the fruit of the Tree of Daat is stated. This applies to the Tree of Daat alone, because this tree only offers the deceptive daat (knowledge) of duality. It says nothing against eating from the Tree of Life. Adam is meant to partake of the Tree of Life; in fact it appears to be his duty to do so.

The Tree of Life represents the sefirotic merkavah that reflects pure creativity and Adam's own image. It reflects the zivug of Adam and his context, the zivug of both Garden and Eden. The Tree of Life is literally the *mirrorlike wisdom* that awakens the mind to its own nature. Through the Tree of Life the mind can recognize open primordial cognizance, and as a result can nullify all separation to the gnosis of Divine realization.

The Tree of Daat is introduced with the words *Good and Evil.* As opposites, Good and Evil represent the ultimate dualistic contrast. The ultimate Divine good is non-duality. This is a unity that goes beyond contrast and all ontological and epistemological extremes. If we call unity "good," a question is automatically posed. The term can be taken in two ways. It can function either as a contrast to evil or as an ultimate disposition beyond fixation to any circumstance or categorical language. When good is defined as the opposite of evil it is reduced to mere lingual equivalency. This is only a state of pleasing beneficence that the mind can grasp. The ultimate good is beyond grasp.

In their dualistic context Good and Evil only exist dependently. One can only be presented in relation to the other. Good is good simply because it is not evil, and vice versa. This dependent relationship only refers to conventional concepts, and therefore says nothing about ultimate good at all. Ultimate good cannot be separate from evil, or from any possibility, and cannot be defined by any relative distinction or circumstance. The essence of good therefore is only Ain Sof.

Digesting the fruit of the Tree of Daat insures that the mind will generate dualistic deceptions. If its fruit is ingested then primordial purity will be concealed; the mind will habitually project endless fictions that reify the assumption that it is a subject perceiving objects that are either real or unreal in relation to it. It is important that the Tree of Daat bears its poisonous fruit in Eden. If Eden truly represents perfect wholeness, then that wholeness cannot exclude the possibility of imperfection. However, seen through the lens of primordial purity, even error is wisdom. Unity means that all possibilities present themselves by a common nature. Its gnosis is the realization of a radically equalizing purity. However, gaining this realization requires eating of the fruit of the Tree of Life, which is automatic if the fruit of the Tree of Duality does not obstruct it.

The Tree of Life offers a visionary pure view that automatically knows what game duality is playing. When the fruit of gnosis is eaten it does not matter if the other fruit is eaten or not; wisdom will be apparent. Every possible variable can be free to present itself, and each reflection will reveal the same essential nature that is bitul to Ain Sof. This is the "ultimate good," which allows the distinction between "Good and Evil" to lose all of its relative meaning.

Daat literally means "knowledge." The sefirah of daat is the connection between *yud-heh* and *vav-heh,* which allows the Divine Image to be realized as a comprehensive whole. Divine daat is non-dual wisdom, so it might seem unusual that this word is used in the context of duality. There are infinite aspects of daat, including the daat of imperfection, which is the basis of ordinary knowledge and its dualistic distinctions. This daat covers over what the ultimate daat presents. Dualistic daat characterizes all things as either "good" or "evil," depending on where they sit in relation to the needs and desires of the ego. Without this dualistic daat, perception would be gnosis. The daat of Good and Evil, therefore, represents the dimming and dulling of the mind's natural condition into a form in which its original condition seems lost. This is what exoteric religionists miss when they grasp at moral assumptions about what the loss of primordial perfection actually means. What we should remember when this issue seems hazy is that it is impossible to "fall" from primordial purity, it is always right there, but it is very likely that it becomes obscured to the point where it cannot be recognized.

In the third chapter, Adam's wife will proclaim: "We may eat of any of the trees of the garden, but the fruit of the tree that is in the *middle*

of the garden we should *not* eat" (emphasis added). This simply contradicts what was stated in verse 2:17, which was a decisive edict only
against eating of the Tree of Daat. But the Tree of Daat is not in the
middle, as Adam's wife presumes. Since the Tree of Life is actually in
the middle, Adam and Eve could have eaten of it as commanded. What
is taken by religionists as disobedience is actually another type of error
altogether.

What does this imply? In order to answer this properly we must
widen the scope of the question. Exoteric religion associates this
error with a state of corruption called *sin*. All the familiar moral bag-
gage is heaped on top of this concept. The codes of behavior, which
identify what a sin is or is not, have contaminated Western spirituality with guilt and shame for millennia. This destructive and
unfortunate set of associations can be stripped away in favor of the
deeper subject of this text: a set of instructions for the cultivation of
gnosis.

From our standpoint, sin is nothing other than the dualistic fixation
that identifies phenomena as a substantial reality. Because of the prolif-
eration of moral fixations, this has gone virtually unquestioned in the
religious imagination. The three chapters that begin Genesis are jewels of mysticism in the biblical literature. Hopefully many more than a
handful of advanced kabbalists will one day make use of these precious
texts in a way that can really point the direction to the "ultimate good,"
which is free of such untoward assumptions.

The error of mistaking one tree for the other is a metaphor for what
conventional cognitive habits do with phenomenal activity, particularly
the activity of the *five senses*. The actual meaningfulness of life becomes
confused with a dualistic parade of reflections that are taken to be real.
The "life" of the Tree of Life is the ecstasy of the play of Ain Sof as it
assumes the infinite self-ornamentation of phenomena. Its structure is
that of the ten sefirot. This is the mirror in which Adam awakens to
the ultimate meaning of the Eden, which is Adam's unity with the garden. However, he must choose and eat.

It was stated earlier that dualistic thinking cannot recognize its nature because it fixates on each mental projection as an object—like a face that cannot see itself without a mirror. The Tree of Life is that mirror. Adam is the living embodiment of its reflexive openness. The text points out that something within the mind emerges to disrupt this innate wisdom. This disruption comes as Adam's wife (the nefesh) mistakes one tree for the other, which suggests the habitual *gross fixation* of the physical senses.

It is important to know all this before it comes up in the narrative, as the commentary has jumped ahead a bit. At this point the dilemma of the senses is approaching. The Edenic duo can subsist on the Tree of Life and abide in Edenic glory as offered, but something emerges that creates an obstacle. We know this from our own predicament. Exactly how it happens is what we are tasked to discover in the text.

The Tree of Life is located in the heart of the garden. Where is that? The garden corresponds with malkut's apparitional space. Space cannot be divided; therefore, the heart of space is wherever we are, in the center of the display of phenomena, in the heart of all that lives. Eating there means literally internalizing the Shechinah's wisdom as it presents itself, in the simple but ultimately profound array of life's appearances. In the moment that this is sought out, the ungraspable barrage of possibility, which is B'reshit, is faced head on. This is food. Failing to dig in and recognize its real meat is equal to eating of the Tree of opposites by proxy.

The Tree of Life corresponds to Eden, and the Garden it grows from is malkut. Its fruit represents their zivug. Its nectar flows from the union of luminous energy and contextual space, which is primordial B'reshit. It is the bliss-filled heart of paradise, the open door to the mind's nature. It is what is implied when the kabbalists speak of lights completely nullified to their vessels.

The life of phenomena is truly an open door. Either we take its circumstances to be cause for endless division, or we struggle to realize a greater intention in the midst of those habits. The imagery of Eden is simply a call for human beings to enter this door. It is an invitation into the innate wonderment of what is right before our eyes. If this is understood properly, the text can function as a direct passage to the Eden we are already in. We would spontaneously realize this if we could only stop our ceaseless eating of the wrong tree, which blinds us.

As stated, the account of the narrative was interrupted at verse 2:9 to jump ahead to verse 2:16 to articulate the pivot point of the chapter: the mistake between the two trees and their cognitive implications. With this in mind, consideration of the verses that lie between can commence. The crucially important verse, 2:10, leads into a description of the four rivers that carry the influence of the Divine Name into the four directions to bestow blessing into terrestrial appearance. The section of text that lists the attributes of the rivers (2:11–15) gives the river's names, directions, and other various attributes. But these verses are extraneous to our intended focus, so, we will return to verse 2:10, which states:

> A river went out of Eden to water the garden, and from there it became four headwaters. (Gen. 2:10)

Verse 2:10 is a synoptic image that restates the whole of the view. This requires a brief review. The second chapter began with the vantage point of *primordial daat,* "before" Adam's manifestation on the earth. This corresponds to the hovering of the Ruach Elohim in the first chapter. Then the text progressed through a description of the Edenic state from the point of view of tiferet, Adam's own perspective, which gave many hints as to the gnostic potential of perceptual motion. Throughout all of this Adam's abiding in primordial purity was implied, as Adam and the phenomena of his "external" world are of the nature of equality. This is where the commentary jumped to a later verse to give foreknowledge of the mistake concerning the trees.

Verse 2:10 is the vision of Eden itself. It emphasizes fluid continuity between the supernal sefirot and the rest of the lower seven. This traces the flow of shefa from the upper waters through daat and into tiferet, in which malkut is incorporated. Its elements are listed here:

Water	Essential nature of Ain Sof (*KaChaB*)
River	Unceasing continuity of creativity (*Basis of phenomenal movement*)
Went out	Connection between upper/lower worlds (*Sefirah of Daat*)
Eden	*State of pure motion and energy (Tiferet/Middle Six)*
Garden	Contextualizing apparitional space of the Shechinah (*Malkut*)

The "going out" of water represents the activity of B'reshit that is expressed through Holy daat into all of manifestation. This is the gnosis of Eden in a nutshell. Although the focus of the Edenic vision is expressed through tiferet, and its appearance is its Garden (malkut), we must not forget that all of it is merely the continual display of Ain Sof. Verse 2:10 is a reminder of the greater picture. It is a window into the Divine glory that is realized as Eden nourishes itself and manifests a garden that is literally self-watering. The *Zohar* states this theme in a very important passage from the *Idra Rabba* section:

Chochmah was engraved to produce a river, which comes out to water the garden. It enters the head of Zer Anpin and becomes a brain, and flows out to become a whole body and waters all the plants. This is "a river went out of Eden to water the garden." (*Idra Rabba*)

This quotation emphasizes that all appearance is wisdom (chochmah). Wisdom is limitless possibility, thus it is encoded (engraved) with every possible variable that the garden can express. This is the guiding power of phenomenal and perceptual motion, and thus it becomes the "brain" of Zer Anpin, which guides his "body." His body is the six sefirot and malkut as well at this stage.

The river's flow is not a linear sequence of motion; it is the simultaneous display of pure chochmah—an explosion of the mind's nature. The riverbanks are projections of the river itself, based on its habits. From these tendencies apparitional phenomena guide its wild inconceivable flow. The symbol of the river suggests the dynamism of B'reshit simply through its continuity and total lack of stasis. As the water "goes out" the creative impulse arises as phenomena, and the garden is spontaneously present.

"On the day you eat from it you will certainly die." (Gen. 2:17)

Death is the quintessential dualistic axiom. It is the heart of the lie that delivers the illusion of finality and separation. If we believe in death then we must also believe in birth. Belief in birth means that faith has been placed in the idea that states of being can really be autonomous and discrete. If it is believed that a being can exist separately, then faith in the illusion of substance and substantial reality is a closed book. The consequence of this belief is that when superficial appearances dissolve, then continuity is over. Its conclusion is that life really is as it appears to be in the most superficial sense: separate, fragmented, and random. This is the poison of the fruit of the Tree of Daat. However, before it is eaten, it poses the ultimate paradox: the phenomena of birth and death appear, and the mind must grapple with that appearance. What type of food this becomes is the challenge that the two trees present.

To human life the fruit of daat represents habitual programming that was not chosen. The habit of grasping at mental impressions emerges from prior habits we cannot remember. How it all began is not the issue. What the Bible is pointing out is that this state of error requires correction, so that the latent potential of the mind can be realized as its primordial birthright. If faith beyond dualistic concepts is cultivated, even if it is never fully realized, then the mind's automatic assumptions can be questioned. This changes the momentum of future habits. Beyond these assumptions there is open possibility, which is the fruit of the Tree of Life. Making contact with this fruit is not easy. It requires arduous resistance. For most human beings, simply knowing that this is possible is a huge step. This is one way that the biblical text can be immediately put to work on whatever spiritual level we are on.

The sublime nectar of Edenic innocence, primordial purity, does not know birth or death. Faith that this is possible is an antidote for the root of all mental poisons. We can aspire to live each moment without having to cling to any notion about what it is or is not. Cultivating this state of surrender is the beginning of bitul, which the Maggid of Mezeritch wrote about when he synthesized the lessons of his teacher the Baal Shem Tov:

> Think of yourself as nothing, totally forget yourself when you pray.
> Only have in mind that you are praying for the Shechinah.
> (*Maggid Devarav LeYaacov*)

Surrendering can mean living devotionally with such depth that only the beauty and dignity that spontaneously arises from Ain Sof becomes evident. This is what is meant by "thinking of one's self as nothing." Our fictitious identities do not give us the attributes of Divinity. Real nobility of mind arises when it is deeply contemplated that human life, and all appearance, is the expression of the Shechinah and nothing more. In itself it is actually nothing.

As self-identified beings, we are under the delusion that we were born and will die. The Shechinah has no self-existence to be born or to die. The words of the Maggid lead to a sweetness that can be lived out in every moment if it is simply not resisted. This is the promise that love can utterly flood all of space with sheer delight (Eden). Devotion in this sense is synonymous with bitul.

This is another way to interpret death—as the death of the ego. But even this can miss the mark, because it implies that there is something there to die. The deepest view holds that the mind is beyond any contrivance, and even in its most deluded state it never departs from that exalted status. Therefore there is always equality between gnosis and the ordinary state of perception. Faith that this is so is very good, but this is not what our lives present us.

As mentioned earlier, the two trees of the garden are connected under the ground at a common root. This symbolizes that the one ground (adamah) can take two distinct paths of expression. This leads to some difficult practical considerations. Ordinary perception and gnosis share a common ground and are of an equal nature, but they certainly do not offer equal value. One reveals precious beauty and the other only creates suffering. Intellectually knowing that the fruit of the Tree of Life resides within familiar worldly appearances is a good start, but it is insufficient to manifest lasting change. The fruit of dualistic habit that we are currently eating must be recognized and replaced with better food. This begins with an honest recognition of the mind's actual condition and an understanding of how its flaws are perpetuated. Only by choosing to identify the defect can the repair begin.

The willingness to search out an honest assessment of the mind's actual condition allows faith to develop productively. Only then can it direct consciousness back to the hidden underground root that is the shared basis of both trees. The single ground with its single root is the door into the ultimate good. Both trees continually offer their fruits, but once ingested the Tree of Daat blocks access to the Tree of Life.

This is the human condition. Dualistic daat continually seduces the mind into the concepts of birth and death. However, at any point, no matter how far the mind has strayed, the unified ground of the adamah can be remembered. This can lead the way back to the Tree of Life and its fruit, and the mind can go beyond its habits to know the essence of creativity directly. This requires that the deception of habit be seen for what it is.

The first message of this section of the chapter is to know the difference between the fruits of the two Trees and then choose to eat correctly. The fruit of gnosis is "a river that goes out of Eden." With its nourishment all the horror and all the beauty can happen, but none of it can change Ain Sof. There is simply nothing there to change.

> YHVH ELOHIM said: "It is not good for the Adam to be alone, I will make a helper for him." (Gen. 2:18)

In verse 2:18 we have the first reference to what will become the *nesira* or "sawing" of Adam from his wife. This begins a description of what happens when human cognition confronts its own presence, and with that, every other phenomenon. Adam represents ruach; his "helper" is the aspect of nefesh. Until the nesira occurs, the nefesh functions as immanent vitality within the ruach. What emerges is that the nefesh, which is malkut, asserts a set of issues that reflect the assumption of "independence."

This is the first time in the narrative that Adam is considered in relation to the idea of another being. It marks a division between the state of primordial "innocence" and the possibility of straying into ordinary conceptuality. This begins the next phase of Adam's development, where the mind's capacity to recognize its habits is addressed. This reflects a basic tension that must be dealt with if Edenic non-duality is to remain stable.

The appearance of Adam's wife equates with the outward

presentation and display of the body and all physical matter. This is the ultimate test of view. In the Edenic zivug, matter and energy directly reflect the primordial union of luminosity and space. Once the nefesh emerges in relation to the ruach, the most volatile aspects of the human experience are unleashed. This suggests that Adam might need to fabricate a "separate" identity in order to confront his surrounding context and even his body. In this confrontation, inner and outer aspects of creativity do battle with one another, and the mind's own creative tension becomes the primary antagonist. At this point the text concerns itself with the questions of the average person, locked in the chaos of conceptuality.

The relationship between ruach and nefesh represents the internal dialogue between a human being's fictitious sense of self and the feeling of its "reality." Within this state the body is felt to be a separate "house" for the mind, just as the mind is felt to be a "house" for its thoughts. This relationship defines how egocentricity usurps perception. However, before it becomes apparent in the narrative, a description of conceptuality in its manner of operation will unfold. It states:

YHVH ELOHIM formed from the adamah every beast of the field and every bird of the heaven, and brought them to the Adam to see what he would name them. Whatever the Adam called each living creature, that became its name. The Adam gave names to every animal, to the birds of the heaven and to every beast of the field, but the Adam did not find a helper for himself. (Gen. 2:19–20)

The next step toward the possibility of straying into the conventional dualistic state is Adam's naming of the creatures. Naming is a conceptually loaded activity, but it also expresses the Divine play of creativity. It can manifest in a pure way as wisdom display or it can be a process of isolating things from open possibility in order to fixate upon them. In the last section it was stated that there is one ground of primordial purity. Human activity consists of two paths that either obscure the Edenic state or lead to its realization (the two trees). This is certainly the case with all names, words, and letters.

In the purest sense, letter combinations assert the potential to manifest the infinite variation of phenomena. There is no problem with the activity of representation until words or names are taken to equivocate "real" things by asserting particular meanings, which are then grasped at. As conceptuality overtakes this process the equivalent meanings lose their connection with the inherent "meaningfulness" of the creative state, and they become constricted into isolated fragments. Human beings "collect" these constricted isolated meanings and try to make sense of them, trying in vain to determine what is real and what is not by making assumptions based on the tenuous data. This leads to an endless frantic gathering of fragments, which clutters the vast expanse of the mind. This is how tzimtzum cuts off open possibility once again.

The issue of naming is brought out immediately after the nesira is mentioned for the first time, before it actually occurs in the narrative. It is a literary pause that is used to inject a consideration of conceptuality at an important juncture. It implies that the nesira stands at the cusp between the two distinct directions. This is the framework from which we must consider the next section, in which the ruach and nefesh will end up in conflict.

(2:21) YHVH ELOHIM caused unconsciousness to fall upon the Adam and he slept. He took one of his sides and closed over the flesh in its place. (2:22) YHVH ELOHIM built the side that he took from the Adam into a woman and he brought her to the Adam. (2:23) The Adam said: "This at last is bone of my bones and flesh of my flesh. This shall be called woman, for from man she was taken." (Gen. 2:21–23)

Before the nesira, Adam falls into an unconscious state in which perceptual motion is suspended. This is the silence of Ain Sof, which is glimpsed between levels. This "gap" does not separate anything from anything else, because there is nothing tangible to separate. Transformation itself abides in the natural space of the "seventh day": the Shabbat. This is the silent fire of the Shechinah that consumes and nourishes itself on its own speech. It is referred to by the Maggid of Mezeritch in the following parable:

> An egg becomes a chicken. There is, however, an instant when it is neither chicken nor egg. No person can determine that instant. For in that instant, it is a state of Ain (pregnant nothingness). (*Maggid Devarav LeYaacov*)

In verse 2:23 for the first time the word "man" is used instead of "the Adam." This indicates the forthcoming transition between the Edenic state and the fabricated identity of a male gender unit. The name Adam will continue to be used along with "the man" to highlight their contrast. The narrative has reached the fork in the road between the "original" state and perceptual conflict.

The woman asserts the presence of all materiality. Her presence is the tendency for all mental events, internal and external, to appear solid and independent. This leads the mind into the belief in the tangibility of *substance*. To an ordinary person the nefesh is the unquestioned presence of the body and the projection of its entire world. The ruach usually moves in accordance with this assumption. This is why Adam's wife leads him into disaster, as conventional cognition is always based on body fixation and material fixation. Through the woman's error with the trees, conventional phenomena will seem hopelessly impenetrable in their density, and thus their phenomenal solidity will go unquestioned by the ruach.

*

The presence of things can appear luminous and open or coarse and closed up, depending on the interaction between ruach and nefesh. This determines how the world is. The nefesh and ruach express universal tendencies, thus Adam and his wife can be understood to display a "cosmic ruach and nefesh" at work.

Holding phenomena to be substantial, internally and externally, is the ultimate challenge to faith. It is quite an insidious adversary. Even hard-won progress and sophisticated mystical convictions can become reified if the gross habits of the nefesh maintain their efficacy. Adam's wife will illustrate how the mind automatically defaults to the lowest common denominator shared with animal life. This unfortunately describes humanity in general terms, and directly expresses what happens as the ruach becomes addicted to a body-fixated sense of autonomy.

> Therefore a man shall leave his mother and father, and cling to his wife, and they shall become one flesh. (Gen. 2:24)

In verse 2:24 the man's "departure" personifies the rupture of consciousness from its origins. The man departs from his "parents" to approach (or confront) his wife and the world around him. There is no clearer indication of the descent into perceptual conflict than this.

The father and mother represent the supernal union of chochmah and binah, the luminosity of space, which the man obscures and obstructs as the nefesh and ruach are taken as functions of fictitious independent existence. The man "clings" to his wife as a sign of his impending fixation. The "one flesh" is a composite of materiality that incorporates both inner and outer aspects, and produces the illusion of selfhood. As the narrative will show, this is accompanied by an inevitable underlying fear and vulnerability. If something is isolated it is always at risk from beyond its confines.

Of course the departure from supernal unity only exists in a fabricated world of conceptual assumptions. It is born of ideas about what we think we are and what the world is. The first step toward undermining these fictions is understanding them. This is what the Bible presents—it gives a reliable picture of ordinary consciousness, which human beings would have no notion of, if not for instructions such as this. For those who are ready to hear it, this teaching is indispensable. As the old myth once said: "To know thyself is to know god."

> The two of them were naked, the man and his wife, and they were not ashamed. (Gen. 2:25)

The nakedness of the man and woman represents the vulnerability and precariousness of human identity. The word for "naked" is *arom*, spelled *ayin-yud-resh-mem*. Its numerical value is 320. This number is part of a profound gematria that requires several other pieces to make its point. When the word *arom* is combined with the number 65, it yields the number 385, which is the gematria of the word *Shechinah*. This implies that between naked vulnerability and the realization of the Shechinah something is missing, and its restoration brings gnosis. What is missing must equal 65. The missing piece is the Divine Name *Adonai* (ADNY = 65), which corresponds to malkut. This is what the woman can reveal, and it is the essence of what her mistake conceals. All Divine Names link a sefirah to its essential nature, and they represent the expression of Ain Sof through their corresponding attributes without obscurity. When Adam begins his degeneration as an ordinary "man," he obscures his affinity with the Shechinah, and he loses his "65." Then he simply stands naked. What a contrast this is to the wholeness that was expressed when Adam became synonymous with the Shechinah earlier in the chapter.

However, this process of degeneration is not yet complete. The vulnerability of their nakedness is sealed, but the fear that lurks in their hearts has not yet been brought out. This will happen completely in the third chapter. Its subject will be the effect that the assumption of independence has on the mind; the existential fear that is the man's nakedness will then cause *shame*. This has yet to take effect. This is the fear that we will be exposed for what we are: a sham of a self-deceit. Although conflict has been introduced between nefesh and ruach, the basic tension between them is still latent and unelaborated, as they are "not ashamed."

4

THE CONSEQUENCE OF HABIT

Commentary on the
Third Chapter of Genesis

The serpent was more cunning than any beast of the field that YHVH ELOHIM made, and it said to the woman: "Did Elohim even say that you should not eat from all the trees of the garden?" (Gen. 3:1)

The answer to the serpent's question, of course, is that YHVH Elohim commanded only not to eat from the Tree of Duality. As we know, this is very good advice. It is quite important that this character has asked the question. The serpent presents the tension inherent within manifestation, which arises between the man and his wife. Despite its popular infamy, the serpent is the great unsung hero of all of biblical literature.

The symbol of the serpent represents the volatility of transformation that animates all phenomena. It is common to both the confusion of the Tree of Daat as well as the blessing of the Tree of Life. Its raw power manifests as the tension between ruach and nefesh in the cognitive sense, and the disparity between energy and matter in the phenomenological sense.

As mentioned earlier, the serpent's body suggests a waveform. Its undulation displays the dance of polarity: up/down, negative/positive, on/off, male/female. Through this continuity, creativity is carried into all modes of expression. It is nothing other than the dynamism of B'reshit moving, the evidence of its innate potential. It is utilized as the capacity to empower and adapt endlessly, to do or be anything, either harmonious or chaotic. It is the wild power that tiferet and malkut share, at once that which is most beloved and most feared.

The serpent can manifest as tohu or it can reveal the zivug of the Edenic state. When unleashed, all the beauty as well as all the danger of manifestation becomes possible. Because it represents such great volatility, it is taken by exoteric religion to represent the lurking presence of "evil." This rather pessimistic view was adopted by religious authorities because it is a reminder that all action carries inherent danger. This evokes *fear*. With fear comes the potential for social and political control, which can impose spiritual and moral domination over human behavior. Because the serpent means so much more than this, we can assert our most important challenges to the exoteric interpretations of the Bible right here.

The serpent is labeled evil by those who hold the concepts of Good and Evil to be real substantial entities locked in battle. This holds them to be independent agents at war within the space of creation. Those who believe in this way do not consider the space in which this war is fought at all. That would only create another war altogether between the contrasting forces of Good and Evil and space itself.

If faith can gain enough certainty to hold that nothing has independent self-existence, then the war between light and darkness can be let go. With this in mind, it should be clear that evil is nothing other than the divisive habits of the mind that arise when consciousness fixates on its own mental constructs. This is not to dispute all the undeniable horror and suffering that appears in the world. Faith that evil has no real existence does not make it all go away, but it can gradually erode the sense of perceptual conflict, which sets fear and panic in the mind. These reactions simply add unnecessary obstacles to any problem. Faith is not a cure for bad circumstances; it is an opportunity to recognize the nature of all circumstances, which cuts directly to their root.

The gnostic understanding of the serpent is a direct challenge to the insanity of moral absolutism. Religious law posits that right and wrong are a closed book; there is no creative choice when morality is frozen solid. It is up to human beings to assert that morality does not need any set form other than kindness and awareness. It can be based on fluid adaptation to every unique circumstance, each in its particularities. The symbol of the serpent represents the untainted possibility of a morality that adjusts to the needs of the mind before any authoritarian code, freed from the shackles of dogma and pedantic convention. If it is not rejected as pure evil, this is what it *can* be.

The symbol of the serpent embodies the disjunctive tension between Adam and his wife, and between Adam and Eden. In the forthcoming section the mind symbolically confronts its own projections, particularly the appearances of matter and the body, which will be antagonistically set against its fabricated view of itself. Conditions are only "good or evil" from this relative perspective. The aspect of mind that makes these designations can only hold phenomena in relation to its own interests. The promise of ultimate good that can outshine this antagonism is about to be covered over by a cloud of fixations assured by the Tree of Duality. The Tree of Life's fruit (which ensures primordial purity) will not even be seen through this cloud, and the promise of stabilizing the Edenic state will soon be lost in a haze of confusion.

The serpent offers the opportunity of conflict as the ultimate test of faith. When the serpent speaks it asks loaded questions, which probe the mind's capacity to face its own tension. These questions are the mirror of the mind's dilemma.

The pure view of the serpent is that it is simply a manifestation of the Shechinah, the living power of Eden and mind itself. This power can nullify or reify, depending on which fruit is digested. As the text implied in the last chapter, accepting reification equals *death*. This is the core of all fears. The serpent's first question to the woman will bring uncertainty as to which tree is which. If she gives the wrong answer (and she will) her direction is sealed: the duo will eat the fruit of duality because of the habit of the nefesh's mistake.

This introduces one of the most controversial gematrias in all of kabbalah. The serpent's name is *Nachash* (NaChaSh), and its numerical value is 358. This is a highly significant number. It shares gematria with the word *Moshiach* (MoShiYaCh) or *messiah*. The connection between the two words leads to the conclusion that the exoteric symbols for the source of utter evil and complete redemption are of an equal nature. Can anything state the mystical view more clearly? The principle that repairs spiritual damage abides in the heart of life's basic tensions and conflicts. Where else could it be? Messianic redemption waits in the heart of life in whatever broken and distorted form it arises in. This is what is embodied by the serpent Nachash.

Realizing Eden in the midst of chaos renders human beings tzaddikim. It requires eating of the Tree of Life, which Adam and his wife never get to do. The serpent offers the promise of this potential in the form of questions. The gematria 358 implies that the serpent is really the wisdom of the tzaddik, calling habitual assumptions into scrutiny. Its questions should prompt celebration and joy in the asylums and prisons of ordinary life, but more often they elicit fear.

The serpent's tension is the raw currency that is spent in spiritual work. It certainly can lead to entropy, but it can also be cultivated into a garden. It could assure the gnostic promise of "a river that went out from Eden to water the garden." The continuous dynamism that binds these symbols as a unity—the river, the Garden, Eden, and its water—awaits the answer to the question of the Nachash. The answer will activate the power that liberates or deludes, and the direction of the NeR will be set into its disposition accordingly.

(3:2) The woman said to the serpent: "We may eat from the fruit of the trees of the garden." (3:3) But from the fruit of the tree that is in the middle of the garden, Elohim said: "You shall not eat from it, neither shall you touch it, lest you will die." (Gen. 3:2–3)

In verse 3:3 the nefesh's crucial mistake is made: the peripheral tree of dualistic contrasts is confused with the central tree of the Divine merkavah. This mistake is not a mere momentary lapse; it represents the sum total of all deluded habitual responses and the full force of their momentum. It represents the whole of human cognitive error. This verse is our introduction to assured mediocrity.

The woman made the mistake because she could not discern what the "middle" of the garden actually was. "Where" it was is irrelevant, because the concept of "place" has nothing to do with the garden's true center. The middle of the garden is the heart of the Shechinah's phenomena. It is the omnipresent "point at the center of the universe" that the rabbis of the Talmud presented to the Athenians. It transcends limitation to any coordinate, and eludes the gross fixated habits of the nefesh. The heart where the Tree of Life abides can only be found when ruach and nefesh are in union. When the nefesh's habits alone lead the way, the lowest common denominator emerges.

The garden's middle is the door into the depth of the Edenic view. To an ordinary human being, it serves as an invitation to replace the concept of a logistical center with the heart aspect of pure space. Making this distinction allows the mind to shift into an appreciation of pure visionary presence, which spontaneously arises beyond location in the midst of any and all circumstances. The a-dimensional apparitional presence is the beloved heart beyond all division, which is the Shechinah. Recognizing that the core of all appearance is none other than this, allows the mind to free itself from dependence on the fabricated concept of "place," which is only the product of the habitual need to become oriented through referring to physical coordinate positions. This reliance upon spatial coordinates is a form of bondage that obscures the vast expanse of the Shechinah. One of Daniel Cramer's Rosicrucian emblems (figure 15) illustrates this by depicting the severing of the heart's cord of bondage to the orb of worldly kingship (three-dimensional spatial logic). Once cut, the heart can fly aloft to become unified with the open purity of space.

When ruach and nefesh are completely integrated they manifest the luminous clarity of primordial union, as chochmah and binah do. This is the state (or non-state) of bitul, which is the key to the visionary heart of Eden. The Edenic zivug is realized (or rediscovered) as perceptual motion becomes indistinguishable from basic phenomenal space. In such a condition all phenomena are the aspect of the *middle of the garden*, as no division defining a subject or object persists. This is the locationless atemporal heart of Ain Sof, in which mind and apparitional space are indistinguishable. This is synonymous with the mirrorlike wisdom of the ten sefirot and the essential nature of the creative process. Realization of this is the key to the Divine Image that obliterates slavery to all dualizing extremes.

Unless it is engaged in the zivug union with the ruach, the nefesh will only pave the way into error. On its own it will only eat the fruit of the peripheral tree that obscures the "middle." The error of the mind taking itself to be a separate self is based on the presence of the body asserting the error of its "independence." This leads the mind to only know its sense objects through contrived associations that set its perceptions at a cognitive distance. The ruach sets these problematic patterns into motion to suit the errant nefesh and they both spiral into error. The fabricated associations are imputed onto everything, including the mind's image of itself. For example, the eye sees a chair, but the raw image of the chair has no innate meaning. In order for the subject mind to think it "knows" the object chair, a conceptual association needs to be fabricated that connects the retinal data to a bank of habits that link all the chair *ideas* and chair-like *concepts* the mind has made. This makes "sense" of the retinal image, which can then

Figure 15
(The Rosicrucian Emblems of Daniel Cramer, *1617*)

connect to the concepts of sitting, furniture, legs—the list is endless.

Conceptual meanings only engender more conceptual meanings. They create elaborate networks that only produce divisions. The process is compounded from data sources (the senses/imagination) that link with the mind's deepest stratum of habit. The deeper base habits manufacture the conceptual linkages. Consciousness reifies its mental objects based on these mixtures, and the habits increase in virulence. An entire world is then made out of these habit-based compounds. Because of this the original sense data are lost, and only corrupted equivalent structures remain. Compounds are heaped upon compounds, both internal and external, and the habit is perpetuated until something intervenes. Intervention only comes from wisdom, which is the serpent's call from very deep within the world of shadows and fog.

As long as compound habits dominate, the mind will not be able to know its nature. Unless struggle against habit is successful it will be covered like a jewel in the mud. The mind will never know anything but its fabrications until a desire to resist arises. This is the mind's yearning for freedom, which begins with understanding two things: (1) what the mind is doing to itself, and (2) a view of something greater. This is why these chapters of Genesis are so vitally important. Data comes into the mind through six gates of consciousness: sight, hearing, smell, taste, touch, and imagination. These are the five senses and the internal movement of thinking. These are the tools the mind uses to make its compound constructs. We can waste a lot of time wondering and worrying about where and when these habits arose. Does it matter? The mythology of Eden consoles religious people because it fabricates a starting point for this process. Rejecting this pseudo-history, it can simply be assumed that this is what we are doing right now. We eat from the Tree of Duality. If these chapters provide the information to get some insight into this process, then we can consider the next step: what we can do about it. Do not underestimate the power of knowing how our delusion functions. Rejecting the literality of the metaphor, we can view Genesis as a mirror in which we can see ourselves correctly. Then we might be moved to seek practices that cultivate the mind's desire to realize its nature. (A discussion of practice in that sense is beyond the scope of this book.)

The serpent speaks at the precipice of delusion and awakening. It questions the woman about the fruit of the trees, knowing one from the other. Its question mirrors the uncertainty that underscores human mental activity. The serpent's question implies: "Are you really sure of what you are doing?" This question anticipates the mistake, and opens a gap for an alternative. This call is the last opportunity for the nefesh to realign itself with basic creative power.

The woman's answer to the serpent adds that merely *touching* the tree will cause death. Touch is a sense that human beings rely upon heavily to prove the facticity of substance. More than literal touch is implied here. It is the touch that operates within all dualistic aspects of perception—consciousness "touches" its objects as a subject. This is inherent in the manufacture of conceptual equivalency. It verifies that the two sides of the subject-object divide both "exist."

At this juncture the serpent makes a statement that typifies the crossroads between materialism and gnosis. This is exactly the point at which the mind's wisdom nature will be either honored or ignored.

(3:4) The serpent said to the woman: "You will certainly not die!
(3:5) Elohim knows that on the day that you eat from it your eyes will be opened, and you will become as ELOHIM, knowing what is good and what is evil." (Gen. 3:4–5)

The serpent is openly proclaiming a gnostic view beyond fixation. This astounding verse poses the ultimate reversal of exoteric logic. It states that death has no absolute reality to it whatsoever; it is just the play of mere appearance beyond reality or unreality. This certainly does not mean that death has no relative meaning; it suggests that death (or birth for that matter) has no ultimate or definitive meaning. This statement is meant to be overtly antagonistic to any view that fixates on appearances. What the serpent is offering is an open door to the questioning of conventional assumptions. The Nachash opens this door by asserting the exact opposite of the conclusions the physical senses habitually make. Despite this, the woman will still cling to her phenomenal fixation. This is meant to express just how insidious and stubborn the compounded habits that usurp sense data really are.

The common interpretation is that the woman is a victim and the serpent is a liar. This logic can be turned on its head. The serpent offers the possibility of something that can mitigate the mistake that is about to be made. This is the real meaning of the gematria 358.

The serpent offers the opportunity of redemption and the perpetuation of Edenic bliss. He is proving that he is the messiah in disguise. If the woman had listened and turned her mistake around, the fruit of the Tree of Life would be easy to take. The serpent has used the Divine Name *Elohim* rather than the composite name *YHVH Elohim* that is used throughout the second and most of the third chapters. This is because Elohim is associated with the left side and tzimtzum. The implications of this are profound. Tzimtzum presents the display of the mind's mirrorlike reflections. The serpent calls into question what the mind's habits will do with these phenomena. Will it default to reified animal fixations or will it rise beyond them? It is a question of faith.

The serpent proclaims that eating from the tree will render human life "as Elohim." Which tree is referred to here is not stated, but is implied. The serpent is definitely talking about the Tree of Life, which goes beyond birth and death and constitutes continual gnosis of the Shechinah. Eating its fruit is synonymous with the nullification of phenomenal attachments, and the obliteration of the identification with the personality and body. This interpretation of the serpent's message was easily found in the early centuries of the first millennium. It appears in the Sethian-Ophite and Manichaean systems, of which fragments of text survive. This material was considered heretical by both church and rabbinical authorities by the time they came to prominence and was (almost) entirely eradicated.

The mind's nature has always been, and will always be, "as Elohim." Eating from the Tree of Life would actualize gnostic realization and would stabilize its potential. This would even reveal the mind's obscurations to be "as Elohim." This is addressed in the text in an oblique manner. The serpent adds that eating of the tree gives the means to "know Good and Evil." This asserts that the Tree of Life's fruit provides an automatic understanding of the game dualism plays. If its fruit is digested then all poisons are realized as primordially pure. Gnosis allows all phenomena, including possible deceptions, to display their essential wisdom-nature. Thus the tree's fruit unlocks the mystery of the single adamah from which both trees grow.

If they were to actualize their nature "as Elohim," Adam and his wife could realize human error at its root and would not fall prey to it. This is what makes the serpent's wisdom so perfect. It addresses both the ultimate good as well as its manner of self-concealment. The serpent simply presents the complete ramification of unconditioned wisdom. Ironically, even as this fruit is offered the woman continues to be fixated on the Tree of Daat, from which she inevitably eats.

> The woman saw that the tree was good for food and that it was pleasing to the eyes, and that the tree was appealing as a means of obtaining intelligence. She took of its fruit and she ate, and she also gave it to her husband and he ate. (Gen. 3:6)

The fruit the woman takes is not what the serpent offered. However, her motivation points to a redeeming desire for "intelligence," which is a distinctly human trait that allows growth to be possible. This is not present in animals, who simply adhere to instinct and species habit. This does not suggest that human beings understand this longing or go about the pursuit of it properly. At its root the impulse to gain intelligence is synonymous with the wish to be happy. This longing is deeply connected to the desire to be free of the constraints of petty fixations. Even when human beings cling to neurotic tendencies, it is always with a secret, unconscious hope that something will eventually break and the natural happiness of open freedom will emerge. This is the central motivation behind all behavior.

It is clear what makes beings suffer: claustrophobic addiction to self-manufactured mental constructs. We also know what causes human beings to ultimately become happy: freedom from constraining habits. This is the sole basis of the intelligence sought in the garden. It is not intellectual prowess; it is the natural gnostic clarity that spontaneously arises with Edenic delight. Therefore true happiness and intelligence are synonyms. This is the imperative behind eating any fruit, even the wrong fruit, as both nefesh and ruach ingest here.

> The eyes of both of them were opened, and they realized that they were naked. They sewed together fig leaves and made for themselves coats of skin. (Gen. 3:7)

Eating of the Tree of Daat renders the ruach and nefesh helpless to the onslaught of dualistic reference points. Because of this the mind is vulnerable to discursive thought, and it manifests a hunger for order, which is ultimately frustrated. This is the naked vulnerability of the ego, which only manifests smallness, insignificance, and isolation in relation to the enormity of space. When the mind takes itself for a subject, then the world of objects consists of all that surrounds it. It stands naked in the face of that momentous confrontation, which dwarfs it and robs it of any sense of security. Only the ego cares or believes in a sense of security in the first place. This is the basis for all egocentric defense mechanisms. Thus the reaction to cover oneself and hide is inevitable, and this is exactly what the man and his wife do.

> (3:8) They heard the voice of YHVH ELOHIM moving in the garden at the breeze of the day. The Adam and his wife hid themselves from the presence of YHVH ELOHIM among the trees of the garden. (3:9) YHVH ELOHIM called to the Adam saying: "Where are you?" (3:10) He said: "I heard your voice in the garden and I was afraid because I was naked so I hid myself." (Gen. 3:8–9)

Hiding is the instinctual reaction to the ego's sense of alienation and fear. Where can it hide? The answer is both internal and external. We hide in the very conceptuality and mental constructs that created the need to hide in the first place. When questioned, Adam can only assert his fear as a justification for hiding. Adam's hiding corresponds to a unique feature of egoism: the sense that there is a "witness" in the midst of the mind's movement. This sense of "I" is the fictitious subject perceiving all phenomenal activity. It hides itself within the complex barrage of habits that it fabricates. The attempt for the witness to try to "master" this jungle of activity defines human conceit. Of course it will always fail. Unconsciously knowing this is the basis for the existential fear that is its constant shadow. This is why Adam and his wife hiding is the archetypal image of the ruach and nefesh, lost and vulnerable, at the mercy of a typhoon of self-generated habits that they cannot control.

This is where exoteric religion seeks out the parental figure of God for protection, which only perpetuates the problem without addressing its root cause. It poses that human beings can "hide in God" through dogma and adherence to authoritarian rule. This unsatisfactory solution can be replaced by contemplating the unity of the adamah and seeking out the Tree of Life that grows from it, which begins as the Divine Image is acknowledged as central to all phenomena. This amounts to taking radical responsibility for the mind and facing the root of fear, and then there will be no reason to hide from anything.

It is ridiculous, even in an exoteric sense, to think that a man can hide from God. This is a suggestion that marks the next stage of Adam's complete maturation, which *does not happen* in the biblical narrative. It occurs as the Divine Image is rediscovered in the course of phenomena. This implies that Adam is a work in progress, as human beings are, caught between the tyranny of habit and awakening.

> And He said: "Who told you you were naked? From the Tree that I commanded you not to eat from, have you eaten?" (Gen. 3:11)

Adam and his wife did not eat from the Tree of Daat as an act of rebellion or defiance. It was something that they could not avoid. It was a "setup," if you will. Human beings are born automatically ingesting duality without choosing to do so. This perpetuates the survival instinct of animals, which seek to feed and protect themselves against the hostile outer world at all costs. This stance is completely devoid of the capacity to evaluate its habits, much less their nature.

When YHVH Elohim asks Adam if he has eaten of the tree it is a demand for an account of the condition of the mind. This accounting is a lifeline. To account for the actual condition of the mind is a necessary step in the process of growth. In this and all spiritual texts this accounting must be made. This is tantamount to asking "what am I really doing?" This is the point of reckoning that will allow all cognitive habits to be addressed, and from that the work of repair can commence.

> The Adam said: "The woman that you gave to be with me, she gave me of the tree and I ate." (Gen. 3:12)

When the ruach's movement is confronted with its actual condition, it immediately panics, and then looks to the nefesh. The ordinary ruach is body and matter fixated. Ordinary perception is based in a feeling of vitality that is limited by the assumption of tangibility and solidity. Consciousness is defined by its conception of what the body is and where its borders are. The body is taken to be the ultimate reality, and the proof of selfhood, and the most reliable base from which perception arises. This is the comfort that beings derive from thinking that they exist. It is only natural that the speeding movement of the mind looks to the body when questioned as to what has happened to it. Thus Adam points the finger at his wife and blames her.

> YHVH ELOHIM said to the woman: "What is this that you have done?" She said: "The serpent deceived me and I ate." (Gen. 3:13)

The serpent told the woman the truth about the Tree of Life: that death is irrelevant to the Edenic state. The serpent did not deceive her. The woman deceived herself, and that error rendered the Edenic condition an impossibility for her. Although the serpent did not lie, it did not correct the woman's mistake. This leads to two important conclusions—first, the scope of the nefesh is too limited to abide in the Edenic state by itself, and second, ignorance and wisdom are equal from the standpoint of the serpent. Nachash is an equalizing power that does not make these distinctions. Only the union of ruach and nefesh can express the creative free will that is necessary to realize wisdom when it is possible to recognize it.

Heading into the dualistic state, the nefesh is not capable of accepting equality. When presented with wisdom that exceeds its limitations, the nefesh can only lead itself and the ruach into delusion. The core teaching here is that human consciousness can be presented with the truth of the non-dual nature of the mind, but its habits of dualistic conceptuality will facilitate error until such an unknown factor emerges. This will continue until we are ready to acknowledge this cycle and see it for what it is, then resist our habits with the aid of those who have gone before us. This can only happen when radical intercession occurs from a source of wisdom. Until then, metaphors such as this can illuminate the cycle of habitual deception that ends up in human suffering. Recognition of this is the foundation for future spiritual growth.

> YHVH ELOHIM said to the serpent: "Because you did this, cursed are you amongst the animals and beasts of the field. On your belly you shall crawl, and dust you shall eat all the days of your life." (Gen. 3:14)

The serpent's volatility is natural, so why should it be cursed? The curse implies danger. The serpent's volatility is only a danger to the nefesh and ruach in their "animal" condition. The reactionary animal state is the lowest common denominator of human life. It is exclusively concerned with self-preservation (the basis of ego). Gnosis embraces the danger of transformation while the animal state runs from it. For the evolving human mind the serpent's danger is a precious treasure, which expresses the dynamism of B'reshit through the possibility of change. In contrast, the NeR's dualistic distortion cherishes the illusion of permanence, and is only interested in its fabricated self-interest.

All of the "punishments" symbolize the degradation of vision. The serpent power cannot actually be punished. Its curse reflects how the NeR deals with its basic tension from the view of its dualistic fixation, thus the instability of manifestation is a "curse" that only causes suffering. The curse of the serpent is that it must dwell within the adamah. The adamah is the ground of Shechinah, thus the serpent's "punishment" is to nourish itself, concealed within the ground of appearance. Again, this punishment is only from the conventional perspective. It means that the serpent's wisdom will be hidden, and it will not be offered freely as it was in the Edenic state.

Pure transformative tension is embedded within the way things appear. Appearance is nothing other than this, which implies that all appearances are crucially important even though they may seem common and unimportant. Great care should be taken in what is done with every detail of phenomena, for it is only from there that the "messiah" of the mind's mirrorlike nature arises. All human mistakes and accomplishments emerge from within the same adamah. The serpent's curse is a blessing because it points exactly to where the exploration can begin. The adamah is where the root of both trees is concealed, and it holds the key to the discovery of the Tree of Life and its fruit. The primordial innocence of Eden can reemerge if this tree is rediscovered. The great gnostic message is that it is hidden in what we have taken for granted all of our lives.

> "I will put hostility between you and the woman, and between your offspring and her offspring. He shall strike you on the head, and you shall strike him on the heel." (Gen. 3:15)

This verse articulates the difficult and complex relationship between the nefesh and transformative tension. The antagonism arises as the merciless volatility of change clashes with the human concept of solid autonomy. The ultimate display of the clash between change and the nefesh is *death*. The assumption that there is an autonomous entity that can die makes it seem that the serpent was a liar. From the perspective of conventional thinking this appears to be a reliable position. This is because the nefesh delivers the feeling of raw presence that seems to confirm this fiction. To ordinary beings the body appears to demand fixation on itself, until there is no body left to fixate on.

However, as B'reshit asserts, everything is always in continual upheaval. Nothing remains. Because of this a sense of insecurity between the assumption of solidity and the consuming fire of change is inevitable. This is where the fear and vulnerability that was Adam's automatic response to his nakedness comes from. At this stage of the narrative, it all becomes a curse for the three main characters.

People refer to "my body" or to "my mind" as if these were coins in our pockets. The witness, or sense of "I" that perceives these objects can never be found. As human beings attempt to hold this assertion within an obviously ever-changing field, there will always be a suspicion that something is definitely wrong.

Suffering is assured as the serpent's transformational volatility actually deteriorates the illusion of solidity that the nefesh and ruach cling to. This happens automatically with age, sickness, and death. This is the root of the angst cited by the twentieth-century existentialist philosophers, who were poised between the hubris of logical self-confirmation and the distinct feeling that something must be terribly wrong. It is the nagging irritation that arises from an inability to pinpoint exactly what being itself is, and where its boundaries begin and end. Caught in this existential predicament, we base our hopes in flimsy artificial boundary lines of origin and cessation. When the inevitable dissolution of form occurs, then panic sets in. This is the product of the "hostility" between the woman and the serpent that the text promises.

Hostility between transformational power and body fixation is simply an indication of ego. From the perspective of conventional perception, the inevitability of change is "punishment," and the serpent is thereby sentenced to irritate the sense of safety that we cling to as we desperately try to embrace life as a lie of autonomy.

The verse ends with the cryptic statement: "He shall strike you on the head and you shall strike him on the heel." The statement is directed toward the nefesh (the "you"). The serpent strikes the nefesh on the "head": its seat of control. Within the body's immanent vitality there is a "brain," which is its internal sense of order. Thus the strike to the head of the nefesh is a blow to the organizational logic of body fixation and the egocentric delusion of identity. It is the direct result of eating of the wrong tree.

The woman retaliates by striking the serpent on his heel. First, why does the serpent have a heel? Does he have feet? The punishment given earlier in verse 3:14 was that the serpent shall *crawl* in the dust, implying that he has been cast down. This is analogous to having his legs cut off.

The image of a *standing serpent* represents the capacity for transformational volatility to assert itself just as the Divine Image does. This expresses its stature as the essential dynamic of creativity that stands with Adam and the trees of the garden. Standing presents verticality. The vertical corresponds with *masculine* activity and the *horizontal* corresponds to feminine receptivity. Until it is cast down the serpent in Eden is an assertion of active power. By contrast, when cast into ordinary conceptuality, the serpent "hides" antagonistically within the foundation of appearances. The serpent is then buried in the horizontal plane of the earth, reduced to a concealed agent of conflict, corrupting all of the ego's thoughts about what is real and what is not. From this degraded position the human sense of immanent presence (nefesh) is also dragged down into the "grave" of matter's inert appearance, which is synonymous with belief in death (see figure 16).

By now it should be clear that all of the Divine punishments are only literary devices that describe the consequences of belief in superficial

Figure 16
(Michael Maier, Atalanta Fugiens, *1618)*

reality as a way of life. The woman striking the serpent implies that it is the nefesh that actually amputates his feet. This is not exactly clear in the text. The ambiguity poses the question of whether it is the power of transformation or the habits of the nefesh that are the "cause" of man's downfall. It is not that simple. There is no cause other than the erroneous state of egocentricity itself, which is self-perpetuating and self-dependent.

The serpent's loss of legs is a mirror reflection of his assault on the woman's head. The sense of bodily independence is attacked at its highest point (head), and that attack allows transformational tension to engender a distorted conception of manifestation itself (feet). One follows the other, and the circle of the Ouroboros is made complete. If there is belief in a "higher" and a "lower" in the first place, this mutual attack is inevitable. The feet of the serpent represent its motive power. Its original vertical display manifests as it speaks to both ruach and nefesh. Once its capacity to move is taken away, it becomes silent, and hides in the ground. This links speech with active assertion.

Gnostic realization expresses the power to move and communicate meaningfulness vividly. However, in ordinary perception it hides and does not "stand" for human beings so easily. Thus the future of the serpent, the great unsung hero of the Bible, appears silent, invisible, and impotent. This is the last mention of the serpent that Genesis will give.

To the woman He said: "I will increase your suffering and your pregnancy. You will give birth to children with pain. Your desire will be for your husband, and he will dominate you." (Gen. 3:16)

The "children" of the nefesh are its impressions of immanent vitality and presence in both internal and external forms. In the state of dualistic fixation these impressions lead to the punishment of suffering. Whatever is wanted can be withheld, and whatever brings pleasure will eventually be lost. The body will get sick and die. When its display ultimately dissolves, we lose everything that is grasped, every precious memory, and every link to everyone that is loved. All possessions will be enjoyed by others. All that will be left is the momentum created by sustaining the habits of fixation, which will be the influence that will characterize rebirth.

The text addresses the woman and states: "Your desire will be for your husband and he will dominate you." The ruach is the husband, which is the motion that will spiral the NeR into egocentric identity. The nefesh has no identity without the ruach; it is mere sensation. Egocentricity arises when body logic is assumed by the ruach. The ego is seated in yesod, and there fiction is sealed. Its corruption is facilitated by the ruach's motion as it reflects the hostility that the nefesh and the serpent perpetuate. The whole NeR becomes involved in this folly, and becomes addicted to the notion of its own existence, which is based around an autonomous body image. This dysfunctional bond between nefesh and ruach obscures yesod between them, and disrupts the potential for zivug that could be realized there.

The nefesh's dependence on the ruach for identity is part of the animal survival instinct. It makes it impossible for the body to simply "be" without a fictional identity imposed upon it. This vicious cycle is what deluded beings cling to, and nothing else can be known without intervention.

> (3:17) To the man He said: "Because you listened to your wife and ate from the tree which I commanded you by saying: 'Do not eat from it,' the adamah will be cursed because of you. In suffering you shall eat from it all the days of your life. (3:18) It will grow thorns and thistles for you, and you will eat the herbs of the field. (3:19) By the sweat of your face you will eat bread until you return to the adamah from which you were taken. For you are dust, and to dust you shall return." (Gen. 3:17–19)

It is quite interesting that the curse of the man is actually directed at the adamah. It prompts the question: where does Adam begin and the adamah end? This is really a curse directed at how human beings relate to the ground of perception. It also merges Adam's problems with those of the cast-down serpent, and the paradox it poses.

The ground of appearance is mere phenomena, without any conceptual meaning. The ruach's distortions impute conceptual meaning upon it. This transforms the data of the sense-fields into egoic currency.

This literally curses the ground of perception by cluttering it up. All of these curses are the products of what the mind does *to itself.* The key to the punishment phase of the chapter is understanding the consequences that arise when habit dominates reality.

Even though the habits of the ruach dominate the nefesh, it is the concept of the body that guides that domination. This is why it is written that the man was cursed "because he listened to his wife." The ruach believes that it is separate because the body appears that way, and in turn the body becomes addicted to the self-referencing thoughts the ruach manufactures to reinforce its fictitious identity. This cycle is so tightly woven that nothing beyond its tiny scope can be acknowledged.

> The command that Adam must "eat the herbs of the field" harkens back to the third day of creation where the types of vegetation symbolized three aspects of energy: time-bound energy expended in the moment (grass), cycles of energy (seeded herbs), and the root of energetic expression, which leads to the heart of creativity (fruit trees). The herbs bearing seed, the cycles of energy, are given in verse 3:18 as the food that characterizes humanity in the dualistic state. This implies that humanity will fixate on temporal patterns such as birth and death, harvest cycles, the hours of the day, the seasons of the year, and on and on, until we die. Time and its phenomena engulf cognizance in temporal loops. Fixation upon it insures that the Tree of Life will be obscured. The Adam called his wife Eve (Chavah) because she is the mother of all living. (Gen. 3:20)

Here is where the woman is named by Adam, in the same manner that he named all of the lower beings in the Edenic realm. This reduces nefesh to the status of a "thing." It seals the conceptual domination of the nefesh by the ruach in the same way that mental constructs dominate everything else. However, there is a profound difference: Eve is literally a part of Adam. This holds out the possibility that they can form a zivug when this habit is broken through. Until then, the mind's thoughts dominate the body and its presence becomes a closed book. This is at once both the crime and its punishment.

The name Chavah (Eve) is based on the same root as the word *chai*, which means "life." This is a reference to what the nefesh really is: the Shechinah. Eve is literally the mother-space of phenomena. The truth is that the nature of the nefesh is equal to Elohim. Therefore this designation of "mother of all living" is quite important. It suggests that no matter how severe the domination of conceptuality might be, the innate essential nature of the nefesh can be understood for what it truly is. We can obscure it, but there is no way to "ruin" it.

> And YHVH ELOHIM made for Adam and his wife coats of skin (aur), and He clothed them. (Gen. 3:21)

This is a very deep kabbalistic passage. The word for "skin" is *aur*. It is spelled *ayin-vav-resh*. It is pronounced the same way as the word *aur*, which means light, and is spelled *alef-vav-resh*. In this context, between *alef* and *ayin*, there is a world of difference. The skin that covers both Adam and Chavah is superficiality and cognitive obscuration, which conceals their true nature. Their nature is light, the primordial aur. The word *aur* (with an *alef* as light) is gematria 207. As was stated, this is the gematria shared with the words *Ain Sof* and *raz* (mystery). Recognition of this connection is what is at stake. Covering it over with a barrier of skin is tantamount to blindness and a life of mediocre stupidity. It is what the brit (circumcision) symbolically repairs.

First letters are very important in kabbalah. The *alef*, numerical value 1, presents unity and wholeness, which leads to the understanding of the essential nature of light. This *alef* essentiality is also present in the name Adam (ADM). It can be read as *alef-dam*. The word *dam* (DM) means "blood." Therefore, a human being expands animal blood into the gnosis of unity. This defines what allows human beings to rise beyond the animal level.

The ayin's esoteric symbol is the *eye*. This is one of the most important clues to the entire Edenic myth. The eye is a symbol of perception. This is precisely the function that becomes corrupted by the dualistic food of the Tree of Daat. In its distorted state the eye deceives the mind and causes tremendous harm. It wraps the brilliant space of luminosity in a coat of ordinary skin. This imputes substantiality and tangibility to whatever is seen. This is the final curse the mind affixes upon itself.

> YHVH ELOHIM said: "Behold, the Adam has become like one of us, knowing Good and Evil. Now he must be prevented from reaching out his hand and taking from the Tree of Life to eat from it and live forever." (Gen. 3:22)

This verse states several things quite clearly. First, Adam has indeed eaten of the wrong tree. Second, this has made him "like one of us" (meaning plurality itself). His habituation to the contrast of Good and Evil has identified him directly with fragmented appearances. This is one level of the meaning of the verse, but "like us" can also imply "like YHVH Elohim." The text is ambiguous on this point. Is god multiple? This interpretation illustrates that Divinity is not just an ideal of goodness. It is whole, but as a complete unity it includes all possible variations, including deluded ones. This means that it must include imperfection as well as perfection; thus it embraces the fruit of the Tree of Daat (Good and Evil), just as it does the Tree of Life. This highly esoteric point is crucial to the chapter.

Since Adam has only ingested from the Tree of Duality he must learn the hard way. This is the ultimate commentary on the human condition, which can only grow and learn by trial and error. Preventing Adam from eating of the Tree of Life is a way of expressing that duality cannot just dip into non-duality whenever it wants. There is a long, arduous road to spiritual growth that must be honored. This is the only way that dualistic habits can be mitigated.

The notion that ordinary human beings can just reach out and grab enlightenment is pure fantasy. This verse certainly expresses that struggle is inevitable when pursuing spiritual goals, and struggle with actual dualistic habits is the only way back to Eden. What the text does not mention is that preventing Adam from reaching the Tree of Life is a temporary obstacle, which all the great tzaddikim have proven.

> YHVH ELOHIM sent him out of the Garden of Eden to work the adamah from which he was taken. (Gen. 3:23)

This line indicates exactly what the spiritual work that purifies cognitive obscurations consists of. One must work the ground of appearance as the mind's own nature. This is the essence of the gnostic view. Phenomena and the mind that perceives them are the totality of the work itself. The only way to realize this is not through philosophy or ideas, but through actually working the adamah in every conceivable way. This is the reason that Adam leaves the Edenic state, and it will be the way that he realizes that he actually never left but only obscured what he already had.

If it is clear that his departure was an illusion, then we can all conclude that no one actually leaves Eden. This narrative is written from the point of view of an ordinary human being. We think we have abandoned our Divine origin. We believe that we are cast into terror. These are merely temporary fictions; however, they are very real to us. This is why intense work is mandatory in order to strip the mind of the habits that run so deeply we cannot even imagine life without them.

> He banished the Adam, and at the east of the garden He stationed the CHERUBIM and the flaming rotating sword to guard the way to the Tree of Life. (Gen. 3:24)

The last verse of the Eden narrative describes the forces of the mind that separate the Edenic state from ordinary delusion. This illustrates what is encountered within spiritual practice as obscurations are faced. It consists of *Cherubim,* which are guardian energies of the yetziric realm (the realm of the ruach). The Cherubim are very special yetziric beings. They are directly associated with yesod where the ruach and nefesh are integrated as the brit (covenant or circumcision). The removal of the klipot of conceptual fixation that reopens the gates of Eden is a "circumcision of the mind."

The ruach's realization of the unity of the upper and lower waters depends on the integration of its three central sefirot: daat, tiferet, and yesod. Like the rainbow, the gates of Eden include them all as a composite of function. However, all of these functions depend on yesod, and in a sense, the unity of the whole Divine Image depends upon it as well. If yesod serves as a barrier between tiferet and malkut (Eden and Garden), then no unity can be realized whatsoever, but if yesod facilitates that union then the upper and lower waters join in the complete array of the whole of the Image. Therefore yesod is literally the gate itself, and its angelic guard has a most important function.

One biblical correspondence between the Cherubim and yesod is in the Holy of Holies of the Temple. In that most sacred of spaces there was an "ark," a container where the original Torah of Moses and other sacred items were kept. Over the ark, on its cover, were two winged figures of Cherubim made out of a single piece of gold. These two figures were male and female. When the state of the body of Israel was in perfect harmony and the Divine zivug was being consummated, the Cherubim would be locked in sexual embrace. Conversely, when disharmony and tohu manifested they would turn away from each other. Thus they represented the yesod of the entire human realm.

The Cherubim are situated in the east of the garden, which is the aspect of tiferet. It is stated in Exodus that the Shechinah "speaks" through the two Cherubim in the Holy of Holies. Prophets who have the capacity to bind to the Shechinah were said to draw shefa directly from the point at which the Cherubim met. This is a metaphor for binding the mind to the heart of the zivug. At the meeting point of the Cherubim, tiferet (east) becomes bound to malkut (the Garden).

Concentrating on this point of union is literally a meditation on the union that draws the upper waters into manifestation.

This inner meaning is alluded to by Abraham Abulafia, the great thirteenth-century mystic. Here he quotes Exodus directly and adds commentary. Note that the ark cover is directly aligned with a "tree":

> The Shechinah that dwells on earth speaks to man "from above the ark cover from between the Cherubim" (Exodus 25:22). For the primordial matter of the ark's cover is like the image of a rainbow. The two Cherubim allude to the Shechinah; they are its action and reaction, the male and female. They were forged as a single body with two forms. When they look at each other the Divine Name is between them. All of this was like a tree on the ark cover. (*Life of the Future World*)

Some kabbalists place a single Cherub at the gate of Eden, and align this angel with the archangel Metatron. Metatron is the guardian of the Shechinah's presence in the minds of beings, and is like a gatekeeper in the spiritual realm. This single figure does the job of the two Cherubim locked in sexual embrace. In his most esoteric form, Metatron has both male and female aspects. As Metatron oversees the passage of spiritual practitioners into the inner mysteries of realization, many gates are protected or lifted; however, all of these gates are aspects of the gate of Eden. The name Metatron is numerically equivalent to the name of yesod: *Shaddai* (314). This alignment between the point of union with this angel is incredibly important to kabbalists, and certainly indicates the passage in or out of the Edenic state.

The flaming rotating sword at the gate of Eden is the dynamic movement of the mind itself. When caught in discursive thinking this sword blocks entry into the pure luminosity and space beyond the chaos. The symbol of the sword indicates the discriminative power of the mind, specifically the attribute of gevurah that creates barriers. The sword of the mind "cuts" the shapes and meanings of thoughts away from each other. It also can discern between the path of spiritual real-ization and the path of worldly delusion. Therefore, like everything associated with gevurah, it could be utilized for benefit or harm. The flaming aspect of the sword is another left-side attribute. Fire also dis-criminates by consuming or leaving portions of whatever it approaches. A flaming sword that rotates with the cycles of the mind's patterns, therefore, is the influence of gevurah within yesod. Such an influence prevents the realization of union, and conversely, proper and pure uti-lization of this force facilitates that same union after another manner.

APPENDIX I

KABBALISTIC SYNOPSIS
OF THE THREE CHAPTERS

CHAPTER I: BLUEPRINT OF CREATION
Stage 1: Primordial Creativity

> (1:1) With-beginningness (B'Reshit) Elohim created . . .

1. The word *B'reshit* establishes the primordial nature of creativity. It asserts Ain Sof as the unifying guidance of keter together with its radiant wisdom nature, which is chochmah.

> (1:2) The earth was tohu and bohu, and darkness covered the surface of the depth. And the Ruach Elohim hovered on the surface of the water . . .

2. The "earth" refers to the primordial state of phenomena, which is the malkut aspect of the Shechinah.

3. The raw creativity of Ain Sof is presented as "Ruach Elohim," which is the daat aspect of the Shechinah. From the human perspective, its creative tendencies are "tohu and bohu," the interactive aspects of luminosity and space corresponding to chochmah and binah.

4. Ruach Elohim is the summation of the three supernal sefirot projected as all creative activity, and as such is the basis of the six attributes ("days") articulated in the remainder of the chapter.

Stage 2: The Six Attributes of Creative Motion

(1:3) Elohim said: "Let there be light," and light came to be. (1:4) Elohim saw that the light was good and Elohim divided the light from the darkness. (1:5) Elohim called the light day and the darkness he called night.

1. Chesed (day one): Light shines as a fivefold expression of the primordial Shechinah (*heh* = 5). This is observed in the five mentions of the word *aur* (light) in the text.

(1:6) Elohim said: "Let there be a space in the midst of the waters, and let it divide between waters and waters." (1:7) Elohim made the space and divided the waters, which were beneath the space from the waters, which were above the space, and it became so. (1:8) Elohim called the space heaven. It became evening and morning, day two.

2. Gevurah (day two): fivefold intervals articulate the creative structure of phenomena. This is observed in the five mentions of the contrasting words *rakia* (interval, space, or expanse) and *mayim* (water) in the text.

(1:10) Elohim called the dryness "earth" and the gathering of waters he called "seas," and Elohim saw that it was good. (1:11) Elohim said: "Let the earth sprout grass, seed yielding herbs, and fruit trees bearing fruit of its kind with its seed within it upon the earth," and it became so.

3. Tiferet (day three): The apparitional tendencies of fixity (dry land) and volatility (seas) are presented. The metaphor of vegetation expresses

this contrasting power in three energetic stages (grass, herbs with seed, fruit trees).

(1:14) "Let there be lights in the space of the heaven . . ."

4. Netzach (day four): Expansive luminosity is expressed in relative differentiated form as "lights."

(1:24) "Let the earth bring forth living creatures . . ."

5. Hod (day five): The differentiation of modes of consciousness (creatures) is asserted relative to the human perspective. This is symbolized by mental states that go beyond human capacities (birds) and those subconscious impulses that lurk as influences below it (sea creatures).

(1:26) "Let us make Adam in our image and likeness . . ."

6. Yesod (day six): The integration of all six days within the contextualizing space of malkut occurs through yesod. This is where the complete Divine Image is revealed as the union of motion and space: the blueprint of the creative process. This is reflected in the gematria of YHVH (26), which is equal to the verse number (1:26).

CHAPTER 2: THE EDENIC STATE

Stage 1: The Ground of Appearance
(From the Perspective of Daat)

(2:3) Elohim blessed the seventh day and declared it to be Holy, for on it he abstained from all the work Elohim created . . .

1. Malkut (day seven): The cessation of activity on day seven is associated with the primordial "rest" of Ain Sof. This is the Holy pregnant space of Shechinah, which asserts binah and malkut as essentially equal.

> (2:4) This is the history of the heaven and the earth
> when they were created, on the day that YHVH Elohim
> created earth and heaven.

2. The Shechinah is reflexive mirrorlike cognizance. Whatever habits
the mind holds are reflected back as the phenomena of the world. This
axiom is suggested in verse 2:4 in the contrast between the phrases: "the
heaven and the earth" and "earth and heaven."

> (2:5) The vegetation of the earth had not yet sprouted,
> for YHVH Elohim had not brought rain upon the earth,
> and there was no Adam to work the adamah.

3. The ground of all phenomena is symbolized by soil of the garden
called "adamah." This word can be divided in two parts (adam-*heh*),
which are two aspects of an inseparable unity. "Adam" (human) represents gnostic potential: the opportunity to realize the nature of mind.
The *heh* is the Shechinah, which continually presents this opportunity. Thus the adamah illustrates that the Shechinah is the sole means
for human beings to realize the nature of cognizant purity, which is
Ain Sof. Thus adamah represents the inseparable unity of mind and
its contexts. The non-duality of the adamah goes beyond all distinctions of inner and outer, self and other, and god and creation. It is
the complete and perfect ground of realization, whose fruit is the
visionary gnosis of the Edenic state. This unity is taken from the
distinct vantage point of the Shechinah, which is associated with
malkut.

4. The adamah requires "rain" to produce its "vegetation." Vegetation is
the visionary energy of tiferet (see day three), which is expressed in gnostic realization. Awareness is the "water," which brings the adamah to its
ultimate gnostic fruition. Its flowering unifies motion and space (tiferet
and malkut), which yields the "fruit" of the garden as human spiritual
realization.

> (2:6) A mist rose up from the earth, and it watered the
> entire surface of the adamah.

5. The adamah generates the water it requires by itself. Its capacity to nourish itself reveals its complete and perfect nature, which lacks nothing. This is the key to realizing that mind and its contexts are co-emergent and inseparable. This gives the biblical notion that man was created "from the dust of the earth" a profound meaning.

Stage 2: Formation of the Divine Image
(The Perspective of Tiferet)

> (2:7) YHVH Elohim formed the Adam from the dust of the
> adamah, and he blew into his nostrils the breath of life . . .

1. The Divine Image of Adam is the ultimate expression of creativity and wholeness. It arises as an inseparable bond between the life breath above and the self-watering adamah below. The life breath is the kabbalistic "avira" (luminous space) of the essential nature of mind. Its potentiality awakens within the adamah, which is the Shechinah. Adam is the seal, or heart, of the primordial unity of these two aspects. Only from this supreme gnostic coalescence can the Divine Image manifest. Realization of this is the great promise of the human condition.

2. Adam and Eden equally symbolize gnostic wholeness. Their equality nullifies the division between inner and outer aspects of creativity. They are both expressed from the perspective of tiferet, which is a harmony between keter (avira) and malkut (adamah), as tiferet is the equidistant balance point between them.

Stage 3: One Ground and Two Paths
(The Garden and Its Trees)

> (2:8) YHVH Elohim planted a garden in Eden to the
> east, and there he placed the Adam . . .

1. The name "Garden of Eden" refers to the union of tiferet and malkut. The "garden" aspect corresponds to malkut, which is engaged from the perspective of "Eden" (tiferet). Its position in the east symbolizes this (east = tiferet). Thus the Garden of Eden represents the zivug (union) of the kabbalistic personages (partzufim) of Zer Anpin and Nukva, which are tiferet and malkut, respectively. Adam also corresponds to the zivug, as he embodies both the avira (male life breath) and adamah (female earth). However, Adam is specifically the male Zer Anpin aspect, and the Garden of Eden is its female Nukva aspect. Each is a facet of complete unity, and reflects the totality of wholeness through its vantage point.

> (2:9) YHVH Elohim made grow from the adamah every tree that is pleasant to look at and good for food: the Tree of Life in the middle of the garden, and the Tree of Daat [that is] Good and Evil.

2. The two trees of the garden represent two distinct paths that can express the single adamah. These are the paths of gnosis and conventional perception. Neither the visionary mystical state nor dualistic superficiality can alter the adamah in any way. This is because the essential nature of the Shechinah is primordially pure, and is only an "ultimate good" beyond the dualistic contrast of "Good and Evil." In short, from the gnostic perspective, even that which appears conventionally to be evil is actually good in the ultimate sense.

3. The Tree of Life is designated in the "middle" of the garden, which is the heart (lev = 32) of the space of the Shechinah. It represents the essential nature of the sefirot, which articulate the creative process. This is the key to the Divine Image of the human body, speech, and mind. Its central position distinguishes it from the Tree of the knowledge of Good and Evil (dualistic contrast), which is decidedly not in the middle, and thus is "peripheral" to the heart essence of the Shechinah. This distinction is paramount.

(2:10) A river went out of Eden to water the garden.

4. Verse 2:10 is an encoded synopsis of the mechanism of the Edenic state (see chart on page 139).

(2:16) YHVH Elohim commanded Adam saying: "You may certainly eat from every tree in the garden, (2:17) but from the Tree of Daat of Good and Evil you shall not eat from it, for on the day that you eat from it you will certainly die."

5. Verse 2:17 is an explicit edict to avoid the Tree of Duality. It aligns it with death, which is the trap of belief in the appearances of finiteness and superficiality. When duality is "digested," open visionary wonderment becomes concealed, and the trap engulfs the mind.

Stage 4: Creative Tension as Potential Cognitive Antagonism

(2:18) YHVH Elohim said: "It is not good for the Adam to be alone. I will make a helper for him."

1. Adam's "helper" is the vital presence of the nefesh that will confront the ruach in ordinary perception. This will assume the form of Adam's wife, who will arise from within Adam. The arising of the nefesh from the ruach is another indication of the point of view of tiferet: she is only understood from the perspective of the ruach's perceptual dilemma. Their confrontation is the pivot of conventional dualistic habit, which obscures the gnosis of Eden.

(2:19) YHVH Elohim formed from the adamah every beast of the field and bird of the heaven and brought them to the Adam to see what he would name them.

2. As a precursor to the "nesira" (separation of Adam from his wife), Adam gives names to all of the nonhuman forms of life. Since no being has the potential for gnostic realization other than human beings, several things are implied. All appearances, and thus all beings, arise from the mind. Human beings can realize the creative nature of the mind from which phenomena arise. The human mind is inherently creative, and here a link is made between creativity and realization. The "naming" is a creative act. However, naming also can become conceptually dualistic. The difference between true creativity and conceptual habit is the state of the mind that does the naming. Conceptuality is always based on habit, and true creativity (in the highest sense) is without habit. Thus the naming points out the pivot point between the two paths that the two trees represent. This is the crux of the human dilemma.

> (2:21) YHVH Elohim caused Adam to be unconscious and he slept. He took one of his sides and closed flesh in its place. YHVH Elohim built the side that he took from the Adam into a woman and brought her to the Adam. . . . (2:24) Therefore a man shall leave his father and mother and cling to his wife . . .

3. The separation of Adam from his wife occurs in verse 2:21. This marks the point of departure from primordial clarity, which is alluded to in the line "man must leave his father and mother." Here the simple term "man" (not Adam) symbolizes the human perceptual spectrum. The "father" is clear dynamic luminosity (chochmah) and the "mother" is basic space (binah). Of course perception never actually leaves these primordial aspects of itself, but it certainly obscures them and becomes lost to them. This is the beginning of conventional perception, which manifests the dualistic confrontation between nefesh and ruach. This condition persists through the third chapter.

CHAPTER 3: THE CONSEQUENCE OF HABIT

Stage 1: Transformational Volatility (The Serpent)

(3:1) The serpent was more subtle than any beast of the field.

1. The serpent is the creative tension inherent in all manifestation and its modes of transformation. It is the volatility present in all creative relationships, and here stands symbolically between Adam and his wife. As such, it represents the cognitive confrontation between ruach and nefesh. The serpent is contextual energy, which arises as the interaction of tiferet (energy) and malkut (contextual space). Since they are not actually separate, nothing can really stand "between" them. Therefore the serpent can be understood to be an inherent aspect of all creativity endemic to its essential nature. Thus, the serpent is inherent within the supernal interaction of chochmah and binah as well, although there is no symbolic allusion to that in the narrative.

2. The serpent is called "Nachash," which has a numerical value of 358. This number shares gematria with the word *moshiach* (messiah). This suggests that the same power that can awaken the hearts of human beings can also cause confusion and antagonism. Creative tension is such a power. If its essential nature is recognized, then gnosis can be realized. However, if conventional fixation habitually contracts the brilliance of Ain Sof, then endless grasping will continually usurp creativity to manifest endless egoic nightmare scenarios. Life is what mind produces, and its habits determine the manner in which it will manifest. Thus the power of creativity inherent in the serpent stands at the cusp of discernment between the two trees in the garden and the two paths they represent.

Stage 2: The Habit of the Nefesh and the Serpent's Wisdom

> (3:1) It said to the woman: "Did Elohim say that you should not eat from all the trees in the garden?" (3:2) The woman said to the serpent: "We may eat the fruit of the trees of the garden. (3:3) But from the fruit of the tree that is in the middle of the garden Elohim said: 'You shall not eat it neither shall you touch it, lest you die.'"

1. The serpent questions the woman about the forbidden status of the garden's trees. The woman answers by stating the reverse of the truth: that the tree at the garden's heart is to be avoided. This illustrates the tendency for the nefesh to miss the heart entirely because of a habitual attraction toward dualistic extremes. The primal mistake of the nefesh is identification with the body and fixation on the substantial phenomena of the gross senses and the mind's conceptual objects. This is the habit of grasping at whatever appears solid and real. This is where the heart nature of Divinity becomes confused for that which is peripheral to it. This is also where the true cause of happiness (which is recognizing the creativity of Ain Sof) becomes confused for the momentary comforts of the ego. The tangible phenomena that can be grasped at are always impermanent. Therefore the fruit of duality is death, and digesting it always ends in suffering and loss. This obscures the possibility of gnosis, which is the great missed opportunity of human life.

> (3:4) The serpent said to the woman: "You will certainly not die. Elohim knows that on the day you will eat from it your eyes will be opened and you will become 'as Elohim,' knowing what is good and what is evil."

2. The serpent answers this mistake by informing the woman of the truth: death is only mere appearance, and is bitul (nullified) by Ain Sof. The serpent also adds that eating from the tree in the garden's heart

(which the woman mistook for the other tree) "opens the eyes" and renders the mind "as Elohim." In other words, the serpent expressed the truth about gnosis and the transcendence of death. It added that along with these benefits eating the fruit would allow "knowing Good and Evil." This is also true, because if the fruit of the heart is eaten, then one automatically knows all about the mistake of duality. Its game becomes clear, and one knows too much about that trap to fall into it. When the mind understands from a higher position, the lower simply becomes obvious.

Stage 3: The Egoic Sequence

(2:6) She ate, and she gave it to her husband and he ate.

1. The woman eats the fruit of duality and then passes it to Adam. The woman is cited as the initial problem because the nefesh encounters raw sensation before the ruach formulates its perceptual reaction to it. An ordinary nefesh fabricates a reactive stance to whatever phenomena it encounters (such as physical sense data, emotional stimuli, or imaginative concepts). Whatever arises becomes dualized on contact, as raw sensation is assimilated into the presumption that there is "someone" feeling the sensation. The "someone" becomes directly identified with the body's capacity to feel the sensation, thus the body-identified ego is born. The source of this dualizing habit is yesod, where all ego-reinforcing divisions are compounded. Yesod compounds raw sensation with self-grasping conceptual patterns from the lower ruach (NeYiH). Yesod's influence is pervasive throughout the nefesh, and is also present where the nefesh and ruach overlap. The conceptual compound that is formed there is then passed into the higher aspects of the ruach, which reify and grasp the data as an "object of a coherent perception." It can then get quite complex as the ruach forms thoughts "about" what it feels. Each step deepens the sense of being "someone." From their meeting point in yesod, nefesh and ruach form a bond, which fabricates the illusion of an autonomous

reactive self, which enters into a subject-object relationship with all phenomena. The myth of the central "I" in the midst of cognition is perpetuated to focus conventional egoic "experience." When the habitual dualizing tendencies of yesod are purified, the stages of this process all become nullified. Cognition arises as a simultaneity beyond origin or cessation, wherein nothing is introduced by any kind of linear progression. The phenomena of the nefesh and ruach arise as open expressions of Ain Sof, with nothing in the way to impede or modify the display of its essential nature. That nature is then engaged directly as the heart of all phenomena.

(NOTE: The general sefirotic attribution for the nefesh is malkut. However, since yesod is directly involved in everything the nefesh does, this is overly simplistic. The nefesh is the aspect of malkut that manifests a direct link with the ruach through yesod. Therefore the correspondence "malkut/yesod" for the nefesh is more complete and appropriate.)

2. The consequence of digesting the fruit of duality is that ruach and nefesh appear together "naked." This equates with the vulnerability of the ego, which is a reaction to the immensity of the world that is set against it. When the ego defines itself as "real," everything else becomes an "other," which confronts it as a threat. This confrontation is always hostile, which is the root of the competitive survival instinct of the animal world. The underlying motivation for competition is fear, which is imbedded deep within the mechanism of conventional perception. This threatened position is the manner in which the ruach and nefesh confront each other and all phenomena.

Stage 4: The Formation of the Klipot

(3:7) And they made for themselves loincloths.

1. As a result of their "nakedness" Adam and his wife manufacture "coverings" for themselves, which extend to cover all things. These are

the "klipot" (shells) that mask the true nature of phenomena as they are reified and fixated upon by conventional perception. They make all objects appear solid and tangible. They are formed as the open dynamic play of tzimtzum is taken to be concrete and real, which arises as the ego's vulnerability is asserted. The reference to "loincloths" refers to yesod, where ruach and nefesh merge. It is there that egoic duality is either purified or reified.

2. The klipot that cover the true nature of phenomena are referred to as "skins" (this term is used directly in verse 3:21). In a sense, his nakedness defines Adam as being a "skin" himself. In Hebrew the word for "skin" is *aur*. It is pronounced the same way as the word for light. The difference is the first letter of the words. Skin is *ayin-vav-resh* and light is *alef-vav-resh*. Kabbalistically, first letters indicate a primary disposition. Ayin corresponds to the eye, implying perception, which can be applied to either gnosis or to conventional fixation. Perception can obscure light, which is the other *aur*. The *alef* of the word for light has a numerical value of 1. This implies unborn primordial unity. When unity is covered by perception, the cognitive barrier of a klipah arises. Klipot obscure the recognition of Ain Sof and its light, which is the true "body" of Adam. In this way, conventional perception is entirely made out of klipot, which divide an inner subject from an outer object. The klipah is the great wall that isolates the ego and insures the perception of a fragmented universe of separate bits—it is a blindfold.

Stage 5: The Cognitive Outcome (The Three Sets of Curses)

> (3:13) YHVH Elohim said to the woman: "What is this that you have done?" She said: "The serpent deceived me and I ate."

1. When questioned, the woman accuses the serpent of being the primary cause of her dilemma. This suggests that the nefesh can accept

no responsibility for its condition. In a conventional context it is far too immature. The ordinary nefesh assumes that trouble comes at it from the outside, that it is a "victim" of hostile foreign forces. This is how consciousness reacts from behind the veil of klipot it generates to clothe the world. The structure of the ego cannot face the tremendous impact of the serpent's creative volatility, so in a sense it is the serpent who facilitates cognitive dysfunction. The consequences of this are articulated as a series of curses, which are limitations placed on the functions of manifestation. Adam, his wife, and the serpent are all diminished as a result.

> (3:14) YHVH Elohim said to the serpent: "Because you did this, cursed are you from among all animals and beasts of the field. On your belly you shall crawl and dust you shall eat . . ."

2. The serpent is cast down on its belly to "crawl and eat dust." This suggests that it was originally standing. It certainly spoke. The unwritten implication of the curse is that the serpent is also cast into silence. Speech is the ultimate creative metaphor in the Bible. It obliquely corresponds with standing. A vertical is an active communicative gesture. The serpent's original verticality likens it to the ten sefirot, the trees of the garden, and to Adam himself, all being vertical symbolic constructs. When the serpent is cast down it is set into a passive role. The consequence of conventional perception is that the volatility of creative transformation goes "mute" and becomes unnoticed, as if its creative power were an ordinary part of mundane life. The truth is that all things are profoundly extraordinary because of this power. The serpent silently hides itself behind the klipot of "reality." There it eats the dust of the adamah, invisible to normative human concerns. However, within the adamah it secretly nourishes itself and awaits discovery, just as vital as ever.

> (3:15) "I will put hostility between you and the woman, between your offspring and her offspring. He shall strike you on the head and you shall strike him on the heel."

3. The next group of curses set upon the serpent involve its interdependent relationship with the woman. In ordinary perception there is always antagonism between the nefesh and the volatility of change. This can be detected in their "offspring," who are cited in the curse. The "children" of the nefesh are its feelings derived from the encounter with life's phenomena. The "children" of the serpent are the creative assertions of life that can be felt. Neither has any existence except in relation to the other; they are totally interdependent. The text extends this by stating specifically to the nefesh: "He shall strike you on the head and you shall strike him on the heel." The "head" of the nefesh is its organizational principle, which is body-identified logic and its sense of materiality. The "heel" of the serpent is the point of impact upon its capacity to stand and move. The strike on its heel renders the serpent silent and hidden. The blow to the head of the nefesh seals the inherent stupidity of materialism, which is the common human condition that only seeks substantial self-gratification and holds little capacity to enter into the profound nature of the mind.

> (3:16) To the woman he said: "I will increase your suffering in pregnancy. You will give birth to children with pain. Your desire will be for your husband, and he will dominate you."

4. The curses set upon the woman begin with "painful pregnancy and childbirth." The nefesh gestates and gives birth to the reactive boundaries that dualistically divide vital impulses. These feelings trick the mind into the belief that it is an isolated unit separated from infinite apparitional space around it. This habit always causes suffering, because the body-ego is not stable or permanent. Its needs and wants cannot be consistently met, and it will ultimately get sick and die. The curse proceeds with: "the woman's desire will be for her husband and he will dominate her." Although the nefesh initiates the dualistic encounter with phenomena, it is the ruach that determines the disposition of the

human condition. The ruach (tiferet) stands between the upper and lower waters (binah and malkut). It either separates or unifies apparitional space. The vital presence of the nefesh is the servant of this function, even though in ordinary circumstances the ruach follows the body identification of the nefesh. Thus the "desire" of the nefesh to provide vitality for the ruach is truly a curse, because under conventional circumstances the ruach ensures the future suffering of the nefesh. This is the start of a vicious cycle that ends in all of human misery.

> (3:17) To the Adam he said: "Because you listened to your wife, and ate from the tree I commanded you not to eat, the adamah will be cursed because of you . . . and you will eat the herbs of the field . . ."

5. The curses set upon Adam begin with the line: "because you listened to your wife." This has been explained. When the ruach follows the body identification of the nefesh it is drawn into the habit of self-identification. This leads to the next stage: the adamah itself becomes cursed. It is interesting that a curse meant for the ruach affects the ground of all phenomena. This is because all phenomena are recognized through the perception of the ruach. Only animals, who have no capacity to change their condition, rely solely on the nefesh. Human beings have creative free will, which is the exclusive domain of the ruach. The condition of the ruach manifests the condition of the world. Since the adamah is infinitely adaptable, it will manifest whatever is required by the ruach's tendencies. The next stage focuses on how the adamah yields nourishment. Adam must "eat the herbs of the field." This pertains to the second level of energy articulated on the third day of creation (see verse 1:11). It refers to cyclical energetic expression: the "food" of conventional perception. It manifests the cycles of time and the patterns of birth and death.

Stage 6: Adam Names His Wife

> (3:20) The Adam called his wife's name "Chavah" because she is the mother of all living.

1. Adam designates the name *Chavah* (Eve) for his wife. Adam names his wife just as he named all the other elements of his world, implying that the nefesh is viewed from the perspective of tiferet. Everything about the nefesh only ultimately contributes to the disposition of the ruach, which is the pivot point of the Divine Image. The whole account of Eden is a teaching on the nature and consequences of modes of perception.

2. The name Chavah shares the root of the word *chai* (life). This alludes to the hidden nature of the nefesh. The nefesh is actually a direct expression of the Shechinah. In its limited role as a conventional nefesh this is not realized. It is masked by the klipot of body and substance fixation, and the conflict that is produced by the inner and outer implications of cognition. The text states that Chavah is "mother of all living." This allows us to understand that no matter what may arise, each encounter with phenomena is a direct expression of Divine unity. Holding the most intimate presence of our being as the Shechinah is the door to sublime mystical devotion.

> (3:21) YHVH Elohim made for Adam and his wife coats of skin . . .

3. This has been explained. It refers to the superficial defining boundaries or "skins" (klipot) imposed on all objects of the mind.

Stage 7: Passing Beyond the Flaming Rotating Sword

> (3:22) Behold, the Adam has become like one of us, knowing Good and Evil. Now he must be prevented from reaching out his hand and taking from the Tree of Life.

1. YHVH Elohim states: "Adam has become like us, knowing Good and Evil." With the plural word "us," the essential nature of creativity reveals that it is a unity only expressed as infinite diversity. This is the primordial paradox. However, here it applies to the conventional ruach, which reacts to apparitional diversity with an endless stream of fixation. This displaces the heart of unity, and all that remains from that point of view are the endless contrasts of "Good and Evil." This is a stark contrast to the mystical "knowing of Good and Evil" that the serpent referred to in verse 3:5.

2. "Adam must be prevented from taking from the Tree of Life" is an edict based upon the momentum of natural law. Adam's "taking" the fruit refers to gnostic realization. The natural order of things sustains habit and ignorance, in keeping with the animal laws of nature. Therefore this verse refers to the momentum that perpetuates conventional perception.

> (3:23) YHVH Elohim sent him out of the Garden of Eden to work the adamah from which he was taken. He banished the Adam, and at the east of the Garden of Eden he stationed the Cherubim and the flaming rotating sword to guard the way to the Tree of Life.

3. Adam is sent from the garden to "till the adamah from which he was taken." This refers to the "labor" of conceptuality that is conventional perception. Of course, this labor occurs in the same adamah as gnosis is realized in. This is because there is one ground, although two paths are possible within it.

4. The third chapter ends with: "At the east (tiferet) of the Garden of Eden was stationed the Cherubim and the flaming rotating sword to guard the way to the Tree of Life." The Cherub is the angel Metatron, guardian of both the Shechinah and all practitioners who seek devekut (union). He corresponds to yesod through gematria (314 = Shaddai:

reveals four. Just as *alef* never divides itself in essence in appearing as two, reflection reflects itself on to infinity without ever rupturing basic wholeness. However, appearances suggest the contrary; the world seems fragmented, random, and lacking any cohesive unity. Four therefore represents the inner structure of the infinite: reflection reflecting itself as a hall of mirrors into infinity, yet remaining undivided. In the midst of the reflected reflection is the original primordial *alef,* always at the heart of everything. It is represented as the number five, corresponding to the *heh* and the Shechinah: the open manifesting field of the mirror of B'reshit. This equation is stated in *The Fountain of Wisdom:*

> When you open your mouth to utter Alef you will see there are two: Alef-Alef. Alef-Alef divides into four: Alef-Alef-Alef-Alef. Two at the beginning and two at the end, and basic space (avir kadmon) in their midst. Primordial space is not exactly an Alef, nor is it any less than an Alef. Thus there are five: Alef-Alef-Alef-Alef-Alef. (*The Fountain of Wisdom*)

Reflecting the primordial B'reshit, the diagram depicts the *heh* reflecting itself as two fives, the basis of the Shechinah above and below, which equal the primordial *yud* (5+5=10). Here is the graphic representation:

Figure 18

The next section depicts the name most directly associated with the first chapter of Genesis: Elohim. In this depiction a *yud* is placed over the central *heh* to help form two names, which symbolize the union of chochmah and binah: *Yah* (read vertically) and *Elohim* (horizontally). Their intersection is the reproductive union; the seed of luminosity and the womb space.

Below the horizontal top of the central *heh* is the letter *shin,* which symbolizes the primal fire of the creative process. *Shin* has a numerical value of 300, which is equal in gematria with the words *Ruach Elohim;* the Divine wind/breath connects unmanifest potency and the manifestation of phenomena. It is the Ruach Elohim that literally "becomes" the phenomena perceived by the ruach. It is the essence of B'reshit on the cusp of palpable experience (figure 19).

Figure 19

The *shin* is a threefold construct. This seals some non-dual symbolism. The *shin's* right and left branches are bound at their center. This symbolizes the ends of the reproductive mirror bound at its heart. This is the primal fire that can dissolve the most reified of habits. It is realized in daily life as the alchemical marriage of ruach and nefesh, Adam and Eve, whose unity is either recognized or torn asunder as the mind apprehends the worlds.

The next section represents the application of the mirror as energetic motion. The graphic is based on the structure of the Divine Image, which is the form Adam (the ruach) manifests in the garden. It is represented with the verse *yehi aur v'yehi aur* (light comes to be and light arose). This is a formula for energy reflecting its own reflection, and thus infinitely expanding exactly as the fourfold sequence in the first section does. Central to the arrangement is a *vav,* which corresponds to the ruach. It is in the ruach that the master principle of the "fifth alef " can be recognized. See figure 20.

Figure 20

The last section of the diagram is a depiction of the tzimtzumim: the Shechinah's envelopment within itself. Five rings are depicted to show that the Shechinah is enveloping itself in itself. If we hold to the mystical view we can remember that the enveloping presence is beyond reality and unreality, being and nonbeing. It is inherently free. This is the key to unlocking this succession of doors. But, as stated, tzimtzumim can be engaged either with wisdom or ignorance. Conventional perception experiences them as constant conflict; a confrontation between an internal personal self and alien outer phenomena. This produces a series of klipot that imprison essentiality and lock out the mind that reaches for it. It insures enslavement to the status quo of causal habit, which only ends in suffering as misery.

The gnostic impulse holds tzimtzumim as permeable echoes, which express the open playful eruption of the Divine. It imbues the diagram with its most valuable associations. Two *hehs* appear separated by the process of tzimtzum. Their apparent differentiation appears to divide between an "absolute" aspect (binah) and its "relative" counterpart (malkut).

The gnostic view holds that the Shechinah is an equalizing mirror-like field, which is the basis of all assumptions and perceptions. This is not to say that binah and malkut are the same, as they designate the distinction between the mirror of the basic space and its reflections. However, there is only one field of space, which is easily forgotten, and its essence is Ain Sof. Remembering this mitigates all division that the tzimtzumim present.

Each *heh* presents a *yud*. The binah aspect places it in the uncontainable space above it, and the malkut aspect places it below, in between its "legs." Recognition of the single free essence of space allows us to understand that no apparent state of containment actually imprisons dynamic creativity. Whether it appears imprisoned or not is irrelevant; if we have faith that essentiality is beyond reification and division, then we are free. The mind's essence is the marriage of space and that dynamism, *yud* and *heh*, which establishes the alchemical union that liberates all fetters.

The equalizing fire of realization is represented by the *shin* in the heart of the diagram. This is the primal fire that alchemically distills the presence of creative essentiality from within the fabric of our lives. It is the catalyst that can reverse and dissolve all the reified habits of the ruach. It is naturally awakened in spiritual practice, provided that the view upon which the practice is based is founded upon faith that Ain Sof is the liberating ground of perception and all phenomena.

Conventional habits take the mind in exactly the reverse direction from the pursuit of gnostic realization. It is for this reason that this section of the diagram is represented in polarized form (see figure 21). This is not to imply that we are living in a reversed world of an opposing nature, which would be the ultimate dualistic view. Both wisdom and ignorance are equally available at any time, and what the mind does certainly accounts for the kind of universe we get in the end.

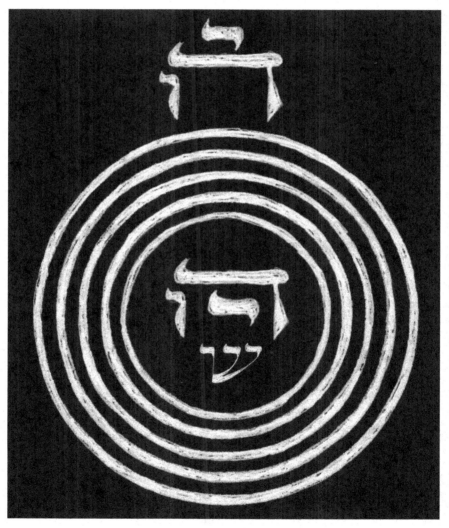

Figure 21

INDEX

Page numbers in *italics* indicate illustrations.

ABOUT THE AUTHOR

Photograph by Gavin Horner

David Chaim Smith was born in 1964 in New York City. His education and early career was as a visual artist throughout the 1980s. In 1990 he began an immersion into the Hermetic Qabbalah, which included ritual work with several occult orders. In 1997 he abandoned visual art for dedication to mystical practice, from which came a unique blend of Chassidic mysticism and traditional kabbalah with Hermeticism. This coalesced through working with the thirteenth-century text *The Fountain of Wisdom,* which he mapped out diagrammatically. The resulting symbol system served as the basis for his 2007 return to visual art. He has held exhibitions in New York at the Cavin-Morris Gallery and at the Andre Zarre Gallery, and his work has been lauded by the *New York Times.* He currently lives in the suburbs of New York City with his wife, Rachel.